Profit-Driven Sales Commissions

Design a Profit-Based Plan that Drives Cash Flow and Makes Happy Reps

Randy MacLean

©2015

Profit-Driven Sales Commissions
Design a Profit-Based Plan
that Drives Cash Flow and Makes Happy Reps

First Edition

ISBN: 978-1508502432

www.randymaclean.com

Table of Contents

Table of Contents 1

Introduction 3

Quantum Sales Compensation 7
    Five Principles of a Good Plan 10
    About Plan Mechanics 14
    About "Incentives" 15
    Steps for Creating a Plan 16

Understanding Profit Drivers 21
    Why Accounting Systems
    Can't Provide Profit Information 22
    How Money is Made — Really 22
    Whale Curves 29
    Gross Profit Production 31
    Cost-to-Serve 32
    Who Controls CTS? 34
    High-Value Accounts 35
    Profit Strategy—10,000-foot View 37
    Profit Strategy 37
    Execution: Tactics Implementing Strategy 38

Creating a Pay Plan 41
    The Sales Comp P & L 42
    Gross Profit Commission Plans 44
    NBC Commission Plan 45
    Negative Commissions 46
    NBC Pay Statement 47

Plan Mechanics 49
    A Tale of Two Sales Reps 49
    Gross Profit vs NBC Commission 51
    Sales Compensation Rates 54
    Base Salary and Alternatives 55

Tracking Compensation 58
Territory Realignment 62
Managing Money-Losing Accounts 63
Transition Plans 64

Designing a Plan 67
Set Baseline Values and Test 68
NBC Compensation Sheet 69
Territory Reassignment 74
NBC Commission Report 77
Benefits of an NBC Plan 79

Launching Your Plan 81
Plan in Private (But Not in Secret) 82
Use Flexible Rules 84
Plan Crediting Rules 86
Use True-Ups 87
Have a Transition Component 89
Communicate Intelligently 91
Common Failure Modes 92
Start Creating Your Plan Today 93

Plan Design Walk-Through 97
Getting Started 99
Picking Representative Territories 103
Examining the Territories 105
Balancing Territories 114
Territory Groups 121
Rationalizing the Sales Force 121
Finito! 125

Conclusion 127

Acknowledgements 129

Glossary 131

Plan Design Workbook 135

WayPoint Analytics 137

About the Author 139

Introduction

This book is a discussion of the considerations and elements necessary to implement a profit-driven sales compensation plan.

Profit-driven sales compensation programs can be extremely powerful tools for company leaders in their fight for superior performance and superior returns. They ensure the sales force is fully engaged in every aspect of the selling and delivery process, reward the people that contribute the most, penalize those that do the opposite, and open new ways to involve everyone.

Profit-driven programs also eliminate the traditional adversarial role of sales management, converting it into sales coaching, where the manager and the rep team up to drive the most profitable sales possible.

The early pioneers of these programs have typically delivered profit rates several times the norm, and these companies have enormous amounts of free cash flow.

Profit-based sales compensation has been the "holy grail" of company owners and leaders for decades, but implementing a truly profit-driven plan has been impossible due to the unavailability of detailed and accurate profit information.

The ERP systems currently in use were never designed to calculate and deliver the granular profit information needed to support these plans, and it is the advent of ancillary systems like WayPoint Analytics that finally make profit-driven incentive plans feasible.

> For clarity and convenience, I'll frequently use the screens and reports available from our WayPoint Analytics system to illustrate how certain information would be used in plan design and execution. In your planning, the necessary information can come from other sources—competitive systems, your ERP system, or even spreadsheets.
>
> The process of developing accurate and detailed costing and profit information is a topic with a much wider scope, better left for other books. Readers with WayPoint Analytics will simply have more direct access to the profit information helpful in developing a refined plan.

In this book, the important elements of profit-driven plan designs are discussed in detail, and the later chapters are a detailed walk-through of a plan for a company with sub-par performance. The use of a low-profit company as the working example is by design, as organizations with profitability challenges need this kind of plan the most, which is a situation where designing a good plan is most difficult.

Some readers may choose to skip directly to the later chapters, roll up their sleeves, and get started — designing their own plan by following the steps outlined there. This may require a leap of faith, as the reasoning and logic from the earlier chapters will be assumed and will not be covered in detail.

> Screens and reports used for illustration purposes contain the names of fictitious people and companies. Any similarity to an actual person or company is purely coincidental.

This book is intended to be compact, with no filler—I'm making a conscious effort to make it a quick and easy to read, giving up the revenue and presence that would be driven by a 500-page version. My goal is for the reader to know what's important, and obtain the knowledge and techniques needed to design an effective and successful plan.

Quantum Sales Compensation

How do you compensate your salespeople? How much recent thought has your company put into its compensation practices?

Distribution can be a tough industry, with many companies only netting a 3% profit on their sales. Given how tight the profit margins are, I'm always surprised to learn how little time and effort many leaders have put into their sales compensation packages.

Commission plans are far more likely to be inherited systems based on the industry norms of yesteryear than what they should be—sophisticated pay systems designed to compensate and motivate a sales force tailored to the markets of today and tomorrow, and which synchronize pay with company profit objectives.

Do Sales "Incentive" Plans Really Work?

The incentive aspect of sales compensation exists only where individual reps are engaged in using the dynamics of the plan to influence their earnings. For this to happen, a plan needs to: have a clearly-understandable connection between desired customer behavior and pay mechanics; the rep needs to know how to influence that customer behavior; the rep must believe it can be influenced; and the rep must have a personality that drives extra effort to improve the territory.

All four of these factors must exist in any territory for the pay plan to have an incentive effect that will produce an improvement.

The analytical work I do shows that most companies have commission systems that pay reps to deliver and defend sales that lose money. This is no small matter—money-losing sales are more than half (and sometimes up to 80%) of all sales in most distribution companies!

A vital concept for sales compensation plans is this: **compensation plans price the value of sales people in the selling part of the business activity of providing products and services to customers on a profitable basis (this concept is a little confusing).** This is first priority of any good plan. The *second* priority is for the plan to provide a reward mechanism that can encourage change in how sales are structured to increase profit for the company. The increased profit funds pay increases for the rep.

Takeaway: The first priority of a well-designed plan is to price the value of sales according to their profit value to the company.

If your company is anything like mine, you can't afford to just throw money away. That's why it's important to design a sales compensation model that only rewards sales that bring in a profit. The purpose of this book is to provide you with the insights needed to put together a profit-based compensation plan for your company. These plans are enormously effective in improving sales force productivity when it comes to generating profits, as opposed to the old method of just bringing in any sale. They also can substantially improve a company's overall profit performance.

What is "Quantum"?

Quantum is a term borrowed from quantum physics, which means the smallest indivisible unit of matter. In our vernacular, it refers to the smallest unit of business—an invoice line. This matters because most invoices written in most companies are money-losers. The enormous profit advantages of understanding and managing this dynamic are the key to hyper-performance, and sales incentives that recognize and connect to it are an important gateway.

Hence, the whole process described in this book is most accurately described as "Quantum Sales Compensation".

Outline of the Book

Creating a profit-driven plan requires a good understanding of the profit drivers in the business—the very elements the plan is intended to both reflect and influence—which is where I'll start.

Then I'll discuss Fundamentals and Planning. This includes an overview of our objectives, the principles behind a good plan, and a discussion of the advantages offered by a Quantum Sales Compensation Plan.

The middle chapters will discuss the mechanics and numbers that go into these plans, as well as some tips that can help you avoid common mistakes.

The last chapter is a complete walk through of a plan design—how to work out the best parameters and rates for various scenarios of territory performance, and how to address the most common issues.

By the end of the book, you should know everything needed to design and implement your own plan.

Five Principles of a Good Plan

There are five principles to a good sales compensation plan. These principles are incredibly important, so I want you to pay very close attention to each one. You'll want to refer back to these ideas when you start to design your own plan to make sure that you're focusing on the things that matter.

1. Pay for Persuasion

A good sales compensation plan needs to pay for persuasion.

I want you to remember this: *pay for persuasion.* The purpose of a sales force is to have a skilled set of people who can persuade customers or potential customers to do something different. If they aren't already a customer, that different activity would involve buying product from your company. If they're already your customer, it may involve persuading them to buy product from you in a different way, purchase additional products, buy in greater quantities, or convincing them to do something that leads to a mutual benefit.

Because many distributors have been around for decades, they often lose sight of this idea. All too often, pay for sales people has more to do with tradition and history than anything practical and productive. So instead of paying somebody to go out and generate new business, these companies will pay people to "maintain relationships" and just keep things going. A company should not be paying a salesperson thousands in commissions just to keep accounts active, because that's not selling, that's just glorified account maintenance. They could hire a dedicated customer service representative on a modest salary to do that kind of work. (The customer would most likely get better service, too.)

Your salespeople shouldn't act like landlords and just show up at the customer's door on the first of the month to collect a new order and get a big, fat commission check for doing so! A salesperson's job is to sell. Their entire purpose is to change the nature of a territory, to bring in new accounts, and new business from existing accounts. Make sure that you're paying salespeople to persuade customers (and prospects) to change their behavior or buying habits. Don't encourage (and pay) your salespeople to just watch the same orders arrive from the same customers month after month.

2. Protect the Best Reps

The second principle of a well-designed plan is that it protects the best reps. When I say best reps, I'm not necessarily talking about the reps who have been there the longest (although they certainly can be the best reps), nor am I talking about the reps who might be overseeing the best territories. Instead, I'm thinking specifically of the reps who do the most to produce new profits for the business. These are the people who are going to help the company meet its objectives, and help the company grow. They're going to produce increased profitability, increased cash flow, and an increased ability to fund initiatives and service offerings that will lead to even more profitable business.

These reps will give you a better future and help guarantee the safety and security of all the stakeholders in the company, from the company's owners right down to the employees with wage or salaried jobs who would like their jobs to continue.

A good plan will not only protect and enhance the earnings of the best reps, but it will help you to identify the people making the biggest contribution to the company. Those individuals will continue to be rewarded as they are now (or will receive even greater rewards), and the salespeople who improve their performance will be rewarded as well in a well-designed plan.

I'll discuss some additional details later, but just be aware that no productive, profit-generating rep should ever be harmed by a well-designed plan.

3. Prevent Runaway Earnings

Some companies have implemented sales compensation packages that don't cover all the possible or likely scenarios. This kind of an oversight won't be noticed until somebody walks in with some giant sale and, under their plan, the salesman would walk away a millionaire. This can be problematic when the company can't afford to pay out that kind of a commission, often because the sale doesn't carry enough profitability.

A good sales compensation plan will prevent runaway earnings. It will anticipate that rare windfall and ensure that the profits generated by that sale are shared appropriately between the sales rep and the company.

4. Operate Within Budget

The fourth principle is that the plan needs to operate within budget. One of the issues that I see with an improperly tested plan is the company may wind up rewarding people in the wrong areas or for doing the wrong things. Subsequently, the plan costs the company more than was anticipated, which can deeply affect the profitability of company.

For a distribution company running a nominal 3-4% NBT, only three of four cents of every dollar that comes in as revenue makes it to the bottom line. If some error in the plan causes the compensation to scale up beyond the profits and, if instead of handing out your traditional sales compensation of $2.5M on sales of $25M, you're paying out four or five million, the compensation plan will likely cause difficulty for the company and its finances. A good plan should always pay for any performance improvements strictly through increased profitability.

5. Provide Performance Insurance

Finally, a well-designed plan will provide performance insurance for the management of the company. A good plan is able to anticipate that some people will underperform, but will have built-in mechanisms to incent other people to over-perform so they make up the numbers.

Can you relate to the following situation? A company with several branches has a few branches that are doing very well. The managers of those branches are doing everything right and have their salespeople turning over rocks looking for new customers, new opportunities with existing customers, and so on. As such, those managers are being compensated handsomely for their work. However, a few of the other branches are having a mediocre year. Under a traditional plan—one with no mechanism to compensate for the inevitable under-performance that occurs somewhere within the business—this would mean that regional management, the district management, and the company president wouldn't meet their own objectives.

A good plan, however, will overcome that under-performance by encouraging over-performance in the successful areas of the business to a far greater degree, which should offset the under-performing sectors. This practically guarantees that the company management will continue to look good to the bank or finance sources, to the stakeholders of the company, and that the senior managers of the company will always meet their objectives and meet or exceed their goals.

Remember: When you're putting together your own plan, you want to keep those five principles in mind. They're the cornerstones of a well-designed and well-executed plan.

About Plan Mechanics

The finished plan will have one or more components that deliver a specific pay amount for a given performance. The components will most commonly fall into three categories: base pay; production pay; and add-ons.

Pay plans may have any number of these components, and each will have its own weight in the total pay package.

Base Pay

Base pay is a regular pay amount that is fixed for each pay period. Base has a number of social and mathematical purposes.

First, it provides a measure of pay security for the rep by creating a floor, or minimum amount for monthly pay.

It also creates a smoothing of month-to-month pay for business that is highly variable, or has a long contact-to-sale cycle.

Production Pay

A production measure is the pay component that scales with the profit value of the sale. The most commonly-used production measure is commissions.

Add-Ons

Add-ons are additional pay that may or may not be tied to specific activities or accomplishments. The most common examples of add-ons are: periodic bonuses; sales spiffs; and key performance indicators (KPIs).

About "Incentives"

When designing a plan, it's very important to remember that the incentives created by the plan are of secondary importance to the real purpose: *to scale pay according to profit value of the sale to the company*.

Whether a particular pay plan operates as an incentive is purely a function of individual reps deciding to exploit the plan mechanics to increase their earnings.

Meeting an expectation that pay mechanics will have a universal effect on individual sales and customer interactions will be highly dependent on the nature of the mechanic and the nature of the sales force.

Takeaway: A pay plan is ultimately a reflection of what the company is willing to pay for sales with a given cost and profit profile. The incentive benefit is secondary, and will depend entirely on how each individual sales rep decides to respond.

Steps for Creating a Plan

Now, with those principles in mind, it's time to establish a framework for designing and implementing your plan.

1. Designing a Plan

The first step on the road to a fully-implemented plan involves actually designing the plan. Start by gathering information about how your current plan works, including current compensation practices, company-wide performance, and profitability.

For those using WayPoint Analytics, you should already have excellent information on Net Before Compensation (or NBC), which I'll discuss in detail later in this chapter. WayPoint will also give you a good indicator of which territories, kinds of customers, and kinds of products make the most money for the company. Conversely, you'll also learn which do the opposite. This information will be invaluable in helping to decide your company's overall direction.

Keep in mind that I'm always looking to *drive change*. My objective will always be to improve the company and the bottom line. This involves shifting the focus of the people driving the sales process so the sales team is working on bringing in the most profitable or productive business. This means that I first need to identify the business activities and customers which make the biggest profit contribution, as well as the ones that make a negative contribution. Only then will I be able to change the ratio of money-making to money-losing business, and work to turn the money-losing business around.

Within your business, you probably have a lot of money-making transactions occurring at this very moment, but if you have an average profit line, that means an almost equal-sized amount of business is draining those profits right off the bottom line. The numbers can be staggering. Most companies, whatever they bring to the bottom line, started with four to five times that amount coming from the best part of their business, but with up to 75-80% drained away by dysfunctional, money-losing business.

Think about that! By just not engaging in that money-losing business, your company would come out much further ahead. This is why the sales force needs to keep its emphasis on profitable business. By doing so, you can potentially double or triple your company's bottom line.

Companies that have implemented these kinds of changes have experienced tremendous improvements year over year. I've seen businesses, over the course of just two years, bring in six times their previous profit! This kind of potential exists within every company—including yours. There are segments of your business that are wildly profitable, but those profits are being gobbled up by the unprofitable segments. The easiest way to succeed in your industry, to absolutely dominate, is to stick your competitors with these money-losing customers so they're being burdened instead. If you can't turn a relationship profitable, sometimes the best thing is to let that customer walk, because they won't steal any more of your company's profits, or any more of your salespeople's time. Best of all, if your competitors are busy chasing after customers who won't turn them a profit, your salespeople may find new opportunities to swoop in and steal *their* best customers.

2. Test

Once you've designed a compensation plan, you need to test it. It's incredibly useful to identify a plan's flaws early in the process before some unforeseen circumstance comes along and exposes disastrous unintended consequences. Back when I was working at a top sales compensation firm, it was absurdly expensive to back-test a plan. Companies would have to make a substantial financial commitment to have the firm back-test the plan by loading historical data to see what people would have made with their actual performance if the plan had been in place.

However, that's not something that WayPoint clients have to worry about. The WayPoint system is able to show exactly what each rep's pay was, and that information can be applied to the plan. On a rep-by-rep basis, you can find out what each salesperson would have earned month to month, had the proposed plan been in place, and identify places where earnings are too high or too low so you can adjust your plan to prevent such issues.

3. Document

Third, you need to document the plan so that everybody knows and understands the new rules. Your salespeople need to understand what affects (or doesn't affect) their earnings. Your managers need to understand the plan so they can provide guidance to the sales force and deal with whatever questions may arise. You need to be sure that HR understands how the new calculations work so your team is properly paid. The documentation needs to cover these bases.

Good documentation is also important for legal purposes. A well-worded document can ward off potential pay disputes or ensuing lawsuits.

4. Launch

Next, it's time to actually launch the plan. Your responsibility during this phase is to clearly communicate the new plan and help your team understand the new elements. You want your salespeople to walk away with a clear idea of how the plan will work for them so they know what will impact their earnings. Be sure to take the time to explain the company's directions and priorities so your salespeople can understand why this is necessary for the business.

Perhaps, most importantly, you'll want to give them a view to the financial upside so they can see the mutual benefit. This isn't just about the company. Salespeople who bring in greater profits will reap great rewards, usually much better than under the old plan.

For example, one very sharp business operator who implemented a meticulously designed plan shared his success story at the Advanced Profit Innovation Conference. He reported that his sales force, across the board, enjoyed an average $30,000-a-year increase in their earnings by switching to a profit-based sales compensation plan. With the full support of management, they were changing the dynamics of the business by choosing a narrower and richer customer base to serve.

Not only did this business produce substantial increases in the earnings of each sales rep, it also tripled the bottom line of the business in one year. They did that by effectively moving away from over 400 of their previous accounts. It wasn't that the company necessarily "fired" those customers (and, on a personal note, I don't like the idea of firing accounts), but they started focusing on the things that really made the company money. They narrowed the service offering for the customers who were draining the bottom line away and those accounts wound up going to the competition, adding to the competition's losses.

At the same time, the business had a sales force that was freed up to spend much more time prospecting, building relations, and conducting business with accounts that were more in their sweet spot. The change also allowed the company to give better customer service to the accounts they kept, ensuring that those customers wouldn't wander off to a competitor.

5. Pay Calculation

The final element is making sure that the payout system works. The pay calculation obviously has to be in place, but there are additional concerns as well. There has to be a mechanism in place that can compute the payouts in an accurately and timely manner.

You also need a feedback system to quickly catch errors should something go wrong with the plan. I can't emphasize enough how important it is that payments run smoothly. There are few things that can damage morale as much as a salesman expecting a big commission check and have it come out wrong. This can be especially problematic when the system is first implemented and people are just getting used to it.

Understanding Profit Drivers

This chapter is critical, as it lays out the underlying business dynamics that directly control profit. Building on the dynamics, I create a profit strategy that the profit-based plan will directly support.

Working back from the end-state is always helpful in developing an effective path to a goal.

Obviously, the desired end-state is to have the company drive much-above-average profits and cash flow. To accomplish this, the company will have to shift focus and activities toward those customers most likely to produce profits, and away from those that produce losses. It will adopt strategies and processes that support this, and those reps making the best contributions will be well rewarded.

A deep and detailed understanding of what, precisely, creates incremental profits and incremental losses in the company's operations is crucial to the development of any successful profit-generating strategy.

Some of the surprising insights in this section provide clarity of purpose and a direct path to eradicating the profit-destroying traditions and practices of below-average companies.

Understanding real profit mechanics and the analytics required to monitor and manage them is key to designing, implementing and maintaining an effective pay plan.

Why Accounting Systems Can't Provide Profit Information

The accounting systems used in virtually all companies are completely unable to help manage profit. In fact, the core functional mechanics of accounting systems confound our ability to understand profits.

This is because they were designed to aggregate sales and costs into a single bottom line number. Their principle functions are to manage inventory, manage receivables, and produce a single bottom line number for banking and tax purposes.

A specialized companion system that calculates granular costs and profits is required to develop good profit strategies, and to track and manage profits.

Takeaway: Your accounting system cannot produce granular profit numbers sufficient to support analysis, strategy, tactics or monitoring of profit-driving activities.

How Money is Made — Really

I'll preface the discussion with the most important aspects of the profit generation mechanics of a business, and the overall objective of every profit strategy.

I also need to introduce the vernacular of profit strategy used throughout the book. (See the Glossary for a complete list.)

The base mechanism of profit generation is bringing in Gross Profit (GP) and performing the functions the customer is paying for with a lower Cost-to-Serve (CTS), leaving a profit (Net Before Taxes or NBT).

```
    Rev (revenue)
  – COGS (Cost of Goods Sold)
  = GP (gross profit)
  – CTS (Cost-To-Serve)
  = NBT (Net Before Taxes)
```

figure 2.01

The Most Critical Understanding of Profit

Building on this basic structure creates a way to clearly understand the profit dynamics of every enterprise, and creates a framework for solid profit management.

Each sale produces a Gross Profit—the amount left from the revenue after the product is paid for. GP is actually the operating budget for the sale. You can't spend any more than the GP amount on operating expenses (and sales compensation), or the sale will generate a loss.

This is a core concept for all profit strategies.

Now for the interesting part—most sales, in every business, carry a CTS that exceeds the GP! In wholesale distribution, the median percentage of money-losing invoices is 62.5%. This means that more than half of all sales in a typical distribution business lose money!

More surprisingly, those companies that get the money-losing proportion below 50% generate outstanding profit rates— usually 2x or 3x the industry average!

Accounting systems lead most executives to a core belief that every sale meeting a minimum Gross Margin (GM%) threshold makes some additive contribution to the bottom line. This is completely false, yet drives a zeal to get every sale possible, leading most companies to mediocre profit generation (at best).

Analysis shows absolutely no correlation between GM% and profitability. Belief to the contrary is the most debilitating factor in business, and is directly contributory to nearly every dysfunctional practice and initiative.

Takeaway: Gross Margin % has no correlation to actual profit, and is being replaced with NBC for effective analysis and management of profitability.

This erroneous belief is incompatible with any kind of strategy for superior profit performance, and its widespread existence is why the vast majority of companies languish at profit levels at or below the average.

figure 2.02

Every productive profit strategy will, in effect, aim to properly balance GP production with CTS consumption, and to drive increases in the spread between these two elements.

Takeaway: Every sale has its own profit-production mechanics. Most sales will tend to produce a loss that consumes profits already made elsewhere. Recognizing and acting on this is key to nearly every profit-oriented strategy or practice.

Net Before Compensation

A new metric vital to useful profit strategies and for profit-based pay systems is Net Before Compensation (NBC). NBC

---

is created by excluding customer-facing sales rep pay from operating expenses, and having a sub-total indicating the profit generated before the reps are paid. (figure 2.03)

This is critical to profit-based pay schemes because it creates a reliable profit number on which to base pay calculations. (It eliminates the circular calculation issue that occurs if the sales pay is, itself, part of the profit total driving the pay.)

It also creates what is probably the most useful profit analysis metric yet invented. Because sales incentive pay is so widely variable—full of exceptions like draws and guarantees, special commission rates, etc.—including sales pay in profit analysis will confound nearly any practical numeric analysis. NBC solves this issue.

	Revenue
−	COGS (Cost of Goods Sold)
=	GP (Gross Profit)
−	CTS (Cost-To-Serve or operating expenses)
=	**NBC (Net Before sales Compensation)**
−	Sales Comp
=	NBT (Net Before Taxes)

figure 2.03

NBC is coming into wide use as a management metric because it encompasses the full spectrum of financial elements that affect profitability—volume, margins and operating expenses —into a single number.

Takeaway: NBC is the central metric of effective profit analysis and likely the best way to monitor and manage profit.

Customer Segmentation

Segmentation is a useful management tool to group customers with similar characteristics. This allows the development of tactics that can be applied to most or all of the members of the group.

For our purposes, it's useful to segment customers based on profitability. I'm most interested in the NBC profit production shown within the segments. This will be used later in the strategy development for the company.

Profit segmentation provides an understanding as to which companies (or proportion of the companies) generate the bulk of profitability within a territory, a product line, or the whole company.

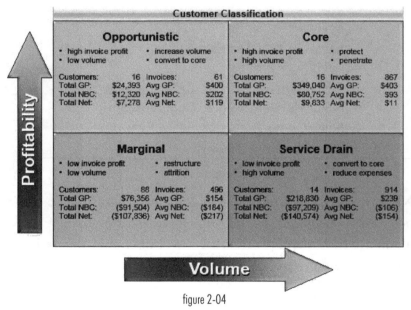

figure 2-04

For the purpose of illustration, I'm using a single sales territory where customers have been segmented by profitability and GP volume. You should immediately notice

©2015 Randy MacLean

that roughly $81,000 of NBC comes from the "Core" group of just 16 customers (the block in the upper-right quadrant). These are major customers who not only bring in a lot of profit on each order, but also buy in great volume. They're customers who you'd wish you had more of.

Strategically, you'd want to protect these accounts and deepen your penetration by finding more to sell to them. These accounts are best in the hands of reps who will work to serve them by preventing and correcting the inevitable issues found in high-volume relationships.

However, as you look at the other groupings, you'll notice that those quadrants aren't nearly as productive. There's an "Opportunistic" segment (upper left) that's bringing in another $12,000 NBC from 16 customers. It's good, but it's certainly not great. If you could get a lot more of their business, you'd be very happy.

The strategy here is to recognize them as a source for future growth, as this is where emerging accounts will be found, as well as large accounts that are giving the company only a portion of their business. This is where aggressive field sales pays off.

The other two segments are losers. The territory in this example is losing over $91,000 NBC doing business with the 88 small customers in the "Marginal" segment (lower left). There may be ways to turn things around and make some of them profitable, but currently, it's business that isn't delivering on profit, and the accounts here will mostly never deliver significant volume.

These accounts are usually best as self-serve house accounts, served via web and telesales. Policy changes, pricing and GP add-ons are most commonly used to address this segment.

Finally there's the "Service Drain" (lower right) segment where the company is losing roughly $97,000 NBC between fourteen large accounts who bring in a lot of highly unprofitable volume.

These are high-volume accounts, usually with logistical requirements that consume more resources than the GP can cover. The inefficiencies affect the customers' own profitability as well, but they may be unaware of it. They'll need some selling effort and perhaps some management attention to turn around.

Overall, this is a money-losing territory. The roughly $93,000 NBC from the profitable customers is being completely devoured by roughly $189,000 in losses. It's difficult, if not impossible, to compete with that kind of a handicap.

If you were to just look at the territory through the lens of typical accounting systems, you'd never notice that you have all of these great customers being dragged down by completely awful business from unprofitable clients.

> Takeaway: Although there are many ways companies segment their customers, to do so on profit potential (GP), and profit production(NBC), is one of the most useful in profit analysis.

As a first principle, I'd like to make sure that I'm not paying commissions to salespeople managing those massive money-sinks. The absolute last thing you want to do is pay to lose that much money. By not paying commissions on these profit-killing transactions, you'll not only see fewer bad orders but salespeople will start to pursue more profitable customers.

Whale Curves

A very important philosophical or analytical device is the "whale curve". It's a great tool for visualizing what's really going on with the profit-generating mechanics in your business.

The visual is the key to understanding the profit strategy I'll be developing shortly.

Whale curves are created by charting the accumulated profit from a profit ranking report. In figure 2.05, the curve ranks customers by profitability, starting in the lower left with zero, then adding the profit from the most profitable account, then stacking the addition profit from the second, third, fourth, fifth, and so on, until there are no more customers to list.

Zone 1 on the left shows customers who generate pretty fair amounts of profitability and put large increments of profits on the bottom line of the company. You can see that $5M of profit is coming in from less than 20% of the customers.

These are the customers that pay the proverbial freight for everything in the company. They allow the company to rack up huge losses elsewhere and still be profitable.

Personally, I think that it's unfair that your best customers are paying high prices and making high margins so that you can afford do business with their competitors in a way that imposes all kinds of costs and drains profits. You certainly wouldn't want to go to a bank to borrow some money and just hand it to the customer, but this is what you're essentially doing by taking the profit from one customer to cover another customer's losses.

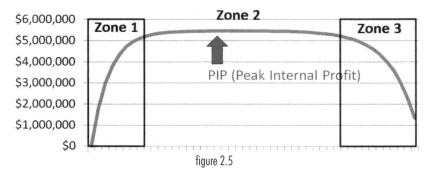

figure 2.5

The thought of burdening your best and most efficient (read: low-CTS) customers by using their much-higher profits to cover the losses you take on their competitors should make you feel a little queasy. I think it's unacceptable. Not just on a moral level, but because it drives you to strategies that make your best accounts vulnerable to poaching by your competitors.

Zone 2 is the middle section that makes up the whale's "back" and consists of small accounts that make or lose a few dollars. These accounts are largely "noise" in the business, driving the need for much of the company's personnel and infrastructure, but producing little or no profit.

Getting to the bottom of the profit ranking, the customers that make up Zone 3 are significant accounts that are losing the company greater and greater amounts of money.

Through the lens of a typical accounting system, you'd see only the $1.3M bottom line for this company. The company president might be thinking to himself, "If we can get 15% more next year, taking the bottom line up to $1.5M, we'll post a great gain!" He'd be completely blind to the fact that there's

$5.5M of profit in the business already, but most of it is being lost to losses from a group of customers receiving far more resources and services than they actually pay for.

> Takeaway: Every company has a whale curve, which will reveal the massive scale of unrealized profit. Just knowing how much profit is available is the first step to setting goals to capture it.

Changing this dynamic can almost instantly increase a company's profit by a huge increment.

For example, if the losses on the money-losing business were cut in half, the profit line in this business goes from $1.2M to $3.5M. That's more like a 200% gain! By doing nothing else, the company would triple its bottom line.

Experience shows that the potential is actually much higher—large-volume money-losing accounts are those most easily and most quickly converted into significant money-makers. The high CTS levels are mirrored on the customer's operations as well, so profit-producing reductions in CTS immediately and automatically benefit the customer.

Most of the activity required to get this done will occur at the customer-contact surface of the business—the sales force. This is why a profit-driven incentive plan is so important—it synchronizes rep incentives and rewards with the company's desire to produce stellar profits.

Gross Profit Production

For centuries, while business was recorded on ledger sheets, revenue was the principle measure of scale and value of a customer.

Computer systems widely adopted in the 1980s gave most businesses the first convenient access to Gross Profit (GP) and Gross Margin (GM%), and these measures have come into more common usage.

For me, GP is a much more useful indicator of account scale and potential. It's a real number that accurately represents the operating budget for a territory, customer, or even an individual sale.

As the top half of the GP / CTS equation, it's the starting point for profit. It also encompasses the first three controllable elements affected by the sales force: volume; pricing/margin; and add-ons like delivery charges or service fees.

All of these elements can have a direct effect on the profit potential of a sale, and need to be considered in a pay incentive plan.

Cost-to-Serve

Profit on every sale is the result of a balance between the mechanics of Gross Profit (GP) production, and the logistical elements that drive Cost-to-Serve (CTS).

In a distribution business, CTS is directly driven by the logistical elements of the operation. In profit analytics, it's easy to quantify the CTS-driving transaction counts that occur in the flow of business.

These most commonly break down to: orders; picks; invoices; and deliveries. CTS directly scales with all of these elements because the more of any of them that have to be accommodated, the more personnel and infrastructure a company will require.

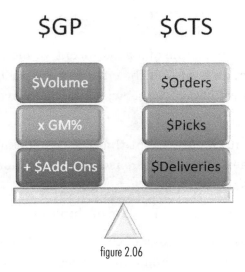

figure 2.06

Managing transaction counts has a direct effect on costs, and is the central priority for companies seeking outstanding profit generation rates. Since this is largely invisible to organizations without advanced granular profit analytical systems, it's also the area of greatest opportunity for profit growth

The principle objective is to reduce CTS per unit of GP. This opens several new avenues for profit growth. Every industry has pretty much exhausted all opportunities for pricing and margin increases, and can get volume increases only through increased market share, leaving only add-ons as a fertile area for GP increases.

Takeaway: Cost-to-Serve (CTS) is directly driven by transaction counts and usually represents the greatest opportunity for profit growth.

However, CTS management has been little managed and offers broad opportunities for improvement.

Who Controls CTS?

One important principle of a good incentive mechanic, is that it must reflect an aspect of the customer interaction that the sales rep can influence. Otherwise, the incentive will be ineffective.

In distribution, the argument that reps can't control costs has frequently been offered as a reason not to include cost-related elements in sales pay plans.

I strongly disagree with this line of thinking.

Of course reps directly control costs! No CEO hires additional personnel or adds infrastructure out of malice or boredom. This is done strictly as a response to the activity attached to the sales coming in.

Costs are directly driven by service models required by the accounts the reps bring in. For instance, accounts that insist on separate invoices / shipments for each department, or place multiple orders each day represent a cost structure less likely to be profitable, and these terms are (or should be) part the pricing of the deal in the purview of rep.

Consider these items:
1) CTS drivers are integral to the terms of the sale—how the product will be ordered and delivered. Logistical requirements are as much an element subject to influence of the rep as are product selection, pricing and payment terms.

2) Pay mechanics are primarily intended to scale pay to sale profit value—the incentive value of any mechanic is completely determined by the nature of the rep in exploiting it to increase their individual pay.

It's important for pay mechanics to be tied to cost drivers. This ties pay to the profit value of sales, and may provide an incentive for the sales force with the intention of influencing the cost drivers as a secondary benefit.

High-Value Accounts

Customers in the most profitable Core group will almost always be those with low CTS% rates (CTS / Revenue). Customers of this group buy significant volumes with a much lower number of transactions than the average.

Put another way, they're the ones with the highest GP / CTS.

Given the prevalent profit philosophy today, where inordinate value is placed on GM%, margins are defended at nearly all costs, pricing policy is unlikely to very closely reflect the true profit value of an account's CTS rate.

This results in an environment where the best organized and most efficient customers produce outsized profit, which are used to offset (subsidize) losses driven by their less-capable competitors, which we also serve. In practice, this could be accurately described as in the following theoretical conversation:

Customer: We need help with more aggressive pricing so we can pursue a great opportunity for both of us.

Sales Rep: Oh, no – we can't do that. Although we make more money on you than any other account, we give the excess profits to your competition, who're so dysfunctional we couldn't even afford to service them without your help.

Although no sane person would actually convey this, it's reflective of the actual practice in most companies.

In a saturated market, the strategy of most players is to flog the sales force to bring in every account and sale they can get. With a strategy guaranteed to load the company with CTS that's driven by marginal and service drain accounts, their very survival is dependent on top accounts providing the profits required to subsidize the money-losing bulk of the business.

A much better plan is to shift priorities and resources away from the profit-drain accounts, shifting any that cannot be reformed to competitors, loading them with the boat anchors that will paralyze their ability to serve best accounts.

Meanwhile we have more resources to give concierge service to top accounts.

Losing the loss-subsidizing requirements of drain accounts allows better pricing for top accounts *without sacrificing profits*. Meanwhile, competitors loaded with more dysfunctional accounts are spread thin, and have even less ability to reach lower pricing levels to win back top accounts.

> Takeaway: A core recognition and identification of customer profit value opens the gateway to an intelligent and strategic process of trading off money losing customers to competitors, while going after their best accounts.

This process is a carefully managed version of the normal customer trading process every company has always engaged in with its competitors. The big difference is recognition of customer profit value and trading wisely.

Fully executed, this can have a devastating effect on competitors still grasping for every sale.

Profit Strategy—10,000-foot View

Working from the information I've gathered, I now know the following about profit drivers:

✓ Most sales add a loss to the bottom line and shifting the usual 65/35 loss/profit balance to a more favorable mix will significantly change the company's profit picture.

✓ GM% is unreliable for profit analysis and management, and should be replaced with NBC%.

✓ The company has sales that fall into three profit-affecting zones: significant profit producers; break-even noise and activity generators; and significant money-losers (whale curve).

✓ Customers fall into the four quadrants that indicate both their value to the company and the strategies for optimizing profit (customer segmentation).

Profit Strategy

This brings me to the most important central objective of the company's strategy. In its end-state, the sales force is working to draw in the most efficient and most profitable accounts, and these will almost always be those with a lower-than-average cost structure, and which are quite profitable at lower-than-average margin rates.

To be clear, high-efficiency accounts can operate at lower pricing and margin levels than is traditionally the case—*as long as the company no longer needs the additional profit to subsidize money-losing business at the other end of the whale curve.*

In this circumstance, the high-efficiency accounts can be attracted and defended with much more aggressive pricing. Our research estimates margins can typically be reduced by 8%-10% (your mileage may vary), while delivering the same or a higher bottom line for the company—*but only if the company eliminates enough of the money-losing business that's currently consuming the profits generated by the higher margins.*

A profit-driven sales compensation plan is a vital tool for accomplishing this fundamental strategy.

Execution: Tactics Implementing Strategy

Articulating my strategy for each element of my analysis helps bring focus to the important objectives that will later drive the elements of the sales compensation plan.

Core Accounts / Most Profitable

Protecting core accounts (accounts from the left end of the whale curve) is the first item on the list for any profit strategy. You want to shift resources and services toward these accounts so you can truly deliver superior service in every aspect of their interactions. This is through the entire range: answering their calls first; first priority on call-backs;

first call on product; heroic rescues; service guarantees; favored pricing; etc.

These will be accounts with lower CTS rates, almost always buying with more product (read: GP) per transaction unit (order / pick / invoice / shipment). Find the markers common in these accounts, and then identify every account in the market likely to be similar and focus on bringing them in.

Service Drain Accounts / Most Unprofitable

The second item in a profit strategy action plan is to correct the dysfunction in the service drain accounts (those on the right end of the whale curve). These are always large accounts with some mechanism that drives up costs.

The cost-driving mechanism may be accidental and can be corrected, putting the account into the core group. If the cost-driver is inherent in the service model of the account itself (big box stores are commonly in this group), you can either shift the logistics back to the customer, or cede the account to your competition, loading them with a money-loser that will reduce their ability to compete on good accounts.

Marginal Accounts

Marginal accounts (the back of the whale curve) are relatively easy to fix with policy changes. The object is to use a combination of service cost reductions (removing commissions, A/R costs, counter costs), and add-ons (small-order fees, delivery markups, a-la-carte service fees) to either make them profitable through increased GP, or to encourage them to defect and drain the resources and profits of your competitors.

Creating a Pay Plan

Creating a new sales compensation plan can be a fair amount of work, and will require a fair amount of commitment to drive to a successful conclusion.

The only reasons for a company to embark on this kind of journey would be to accomplish one or more of the following:
- ✓ re-price what the company pays for a given profit production
- ✓ perform a periodic review and update of sales coverage and sales force size and structure
- ✓ balance territories for best and most effective sales force deployment
- ✓ introduce a mechanism to reward the reps contributing the most profit, and for the converse to also occur
- ✓ get the best reps a pay regime they can exploit to enhance their earnings, to the mutual benefit of both the rep and the company

A good plan will accomplish all of these things, and can be one of the best tools to drive change in thinking, and in profit production.

Traditional (read: existing) plans frequently do the opposite, paying well for money-losing business, and therefore creating perverse incentives for the sales force to fight profit initiatives.

The ultimate goal is simple: you want to cut your losses on unprofitable business while working to increase the amount of profitable business. As you follow the process in the book, you'll notice general trends and markers that can help you identify your most profitable customers, so you can find more like them. You'll do the same in identifying unprofitable customers so the company can avoid collecting more like them. However, by just fixing the unprofitable parts of your business you can expect to see significant gains. With some work, your company can post significant profit gains within a year of implementing your new plan.

The Sales Comp P & L

First, I want to show how to structure a P&L sheet to get Net Before Compensation (NBC). In most P&L sheets there is Revenue, less Cost of Goods Sold (CoGS), which leaves Gross Profit (GP). Then it subtracts expenses like sales commissions and other operating expenses, leaving (hopefully) a positive Net Before Taxes (NBT).

	Revenue
−	CoGS (Cost of Goods Sold)
=	GP (Gross Profit)
−	Expenses
=	NBT (Net Before Taxes)

figure 3.01

Under Quantum Profit Management (and in WayPoint Analytics), the reports are structured slightly differently. There you'll find Revenue, less Cost of Goods Sold, which leaves Gross Profit (GP), less operating expenses (excluding for now sales compensation) which we term as Cost-to-Serve

(CTS), leaving Net Before Compensation (NBC). Then Sales Compensation is deducted, leaving NBT.

For these purposes, Sales Compensation is the gross pay for customer-facing sales reps. It doesn't matter if it's inside or outside sales, if it's somebody that you're paying to convince your customers to buy from you then their pay is considered part of the Sales Comp number moved below NBC.

	Revenue
−	COGS (Cost of Goods Sold)
=	GP (Gross Profit)
−	CTS (Cost-To-Serve or operating expenses)
=	**NBC (Net Before sales Compensation)**
−	Sales Comp
=	NBT (Net Before Taxes)

figure 3.02

There are a few reasons why you want this NBC number. For starters, it's useful to know the amount of money left after you've paid for the product and run it through your entire operation. The sales pay should be kept separate from this number because sales compensation usually isn't a profitability problem.

However, more importantly, it gives you the ability to pay profit-based compensation. The problem with just trying to pay on bottom line is that the sales pay is part of the bottom line; the more you pay out, the lower the bottom line is. If you leave that kind of a circular calculation in place, it's almost impossible to figure out what's going on.

If you isolate it in this manner, the pay plans, which would otherwise be very complex to calculate, suddenly become simple. You can just decide to split this amount with them 60/40, 50/50, 70/30, or whatever the case may be.

Gross Profit Commission Plans

To demonstrate why these ideas are so important, here's a sample of a gross profit commission plan. The red line trends from a lot of real data from companies that WayPoint has helped in the past. While the numbers may change, many companies will have a results that look like this under a typical gross profit plan. There are things like load factors to help protect the company from paying more than it should. Sometimes you'll also have commission clawbacks. There may be thresholds or minimums that keep the company from paying out unless a certain amount of commission is met on a sale.

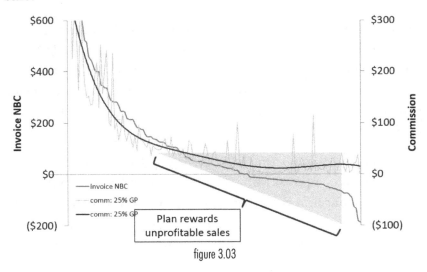

figure 3.03

Essentially here is what happens: As the gross profit on the sale—as shown by the jagged pink line—you may or may not pay a certain amount of commission. (figure 2.03) These entries have been ranked by the amount of commission paid and the gross profit can be greater or narrower. However, under this kind of a plan you would almost always end up paying something; there are very few instances where nothing is paid. That's because the salespeople are aware of whatever mechanisms you may have in place and make sure that they always wind up at least on the threshold of being paid.

The blue line shows the NBC on the sale. It indicates how much money the company has left to split with the sales force. As that line comes down, the company pays smaller and smaller amounts of commission on the sale until I wind up having a profit line continue right into negatives. Effectively there's an entire section of a plan where sales reps are being paid in cases where the company cannot possibly make money, such as the gross profit below about $100 which can't cover the operating expenses on a warehouse pick and delivery. As such, typical commission plans have a huge area where salespeople are essentially being paid to lose money.

NBC Commission Plan

What you need is a commission plan that tracks profitability. You want to pay somebody on a sale, even if it only makes a dollar after all the expenses are accounted for. Conversely, if the sale goes underwater, the commission should go underwater as well. You also don't want a situation where the salesperson can leave the company holding the bag on a sale because that's going to cost a good deal of money. A good NBC program will keep those things tracked.

The other benefits, which I'll expand upon in later chapters, are that such will allow for negative commissions, scale through the performance range, and be very simple to operate.

Using the same sales data set as the previous chart, and NBC-based compensation program tracks profit generation past zero and into negatives. Since commissions can go negative when profits do, the plan is completely reflective of sales profitability, causing reps to share in the losses of bad sales. (figure 2.04)

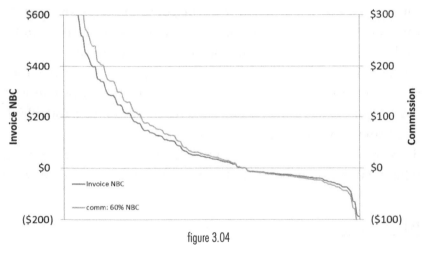

figure 3.04

Negative Commissions

An important feature of an NBC-based compensation program is the concept of negative commissions. The plan will actually deduct pay for money-losing sales.

Historically, companies have attempted to address the issue of paying commissions on money-losing sales using other mechanics, like minimum-margin thresholds and load factors. With distribution companies currently writing a median of 62.5% money-losing orders, it's clear that these mechanics simply do not work. (From our research, we know that margins have as little to do with profits as the phases of the moon, so it's easy to understand why margin-driven mechanics are unable to effectively influence profits.)

> Takeaway: Gross Margin % has almost no correlation to profitability. Any pay mechanic or management method driven by Gross Margin % is unlikely to have any useful influence on profits.

The negative-commission feature is vital to creating a profit-driven plan, and provides the following benefits:
- ✓ it disincentivizes money-losing sales
- ✓ it makes the plan easy to understand and calculate
- ✓ it replaces inherently-dysfunctional minimum-margin mechanics that work against profitability because they:
  - o discourage sales efforts in the most efficient and profitable accounts where high profit is available at lower margins
  - o insert a floor under rep earnings, protecting the rep from the impact of money-losing sales by shifting the entire cost of losses onto the company
  - o disconnect rep pay from company goals, paying for money-losing sales, and creating an adversarial management dynamic, where the company needs to rein in losing sales

NBC Pay Statement

One of the things I really like about our implementation of profit-driven compensation is the pay statement. It not only reports the pay due from each active account, it also shows the rep what unrealized potential was in the territory. (figure 3.05)

The statement shows the commission total due, and also the amount of commission that would have been paid if the money-losing accounts had just broken even. In addition, it shows what commissions would have been if all the accounts below the average NBC profit rate had come in at the average.

400 Anders, Fred								Date: 3/15/2010 Fiscal Period: 201002
Customer	Orders	(NBC)	Rev	GP	GM%	NBC	NBC%	Comm
6981 Interdigital Communications Corporation	1	0%	$78,077	$12,375	15.8%	$10,596	13.6%	$3,708.53
1445 Kilian Mfg Co	14	14%	$25,531	$7,959	31.2%	$6,104	23.9%	$2,136.26
2922 Dynamics Research Corporation	8	38%	$28,057	$5,210	18.6%	$3,932	14.0%	$1,376.34
3489 Disc Graphics Inc	11	0%	$19,681	$4,885	24.8%	$2,627	13.3%	$919.28
6349 12th Street Ht Associatates LP	28	55%	$83,226	$7,853	9.4%	$1,943	2.3%	$680.19
343 Hyde Park Savings Bank	2	0%	$5,761	$1,512	26.2%	$1,089	18.9%	$381.07
4989 Cleveland Energy Resources	1	0%	$1,595	$666	41.8%	$448	28.1%	$156.86
1468 Uniland Partnership of Del LP	1	0%	$1,605	$419	26.1%	$251	15.6%	$87.80
392 New America High Income Fund	1	0%	$1,696	$460	27.1%	$190	11.2%	$66.62
1007 Great Lakes Lithograph Co	1	100%	$234	$64	27.3%	($42)	-18.0%	($14.70)
5262 Tweeter Home Entertainment Group Inc	1	100%	$817	$115	14.1%	($91)	-11.2%	($31.92)
683 Equitrans L P	5	40%	($3,663)	$215	-5.9%	($518)	14.2%	($181.45)
563 First American Equity Ln Svcs	13	86%	$5,791	$1,296	22.4%	($1,301)	-22.5%	($455.30)
			$248,409	$43,031		$25,227		$8,829.59

Customers: 13
Orders: 87
Invoices: 90
Money-Losing Invoices: 41.1%

Gross Margin: 17%
NBC Rate: 10%

Total Commissions: $8,829.59
(if you had no money-losing sales): $11,158.99
(if all sales were at your average profit rate): $11,692.79

Base Pay: $2,000.00
Commissions: $8,829.59
Other Pay: $0.00
Adjustments: $0.00
Total Pay: $10,829.59

figure 3.05

This has proven to be a terrific tool to help managers work with reps to capture profits.

Plan Mechanics

In the last chapter, I discussed the considerations that need to go into a well-designed sales compensation plan. This included making sure that you're paying for persuasion, protecting the best reps, shielding the company from runaway earnings, rewarding the people who make the greatest contributions, and providing performance insurance.

This chapter will discuss the plan mechanics, mathematics, and regulations that will accommodate those objectives. Later chapters will build on these ideas by showing a lot of the actual math that goes into the program.

A Tale of Two Sales Reps

Before I get into how things will be under a NBC plan, let's take a look at how things are right now by comparing two sales reps under a traditional compensation plan. The first rep whose performance I'm going to look at is named Minh Fuller. Minh's a younger guy, but he's been around for a while and is a real go-getter. Minh generates $190,000 in gross profit (I'm not going to look at his revenue because, unlike gross profit dollars, it's not all that relevant in terms of producing profit for the company). It costs about about $65,000 to pay for all of our operating expenses for his business, after which I have $125,000 remaining. Minh is paid around \$73,000 which to about 58.8% or 59% of the NBC. (figure 4.05)

As discussed in the previous chapter, the NBC number is useful because it represents the money left after paying for the product and the operational costs to deliver it to the customer. This is the amount of money that the company splits with Minh. Minh is receiving roughly 60% of the NBC that he's generating, which is fairly typical in wholesale distribution. Anywhere between 40% to 60% of the NBC generated gets paid out to the sales rep in a profitable territory. Minh is getting paid a base plus commission and, since the commission is based on the gross profit, this is how it works out.

Rep	Invoices	Revenue	GP		Net		NBC		Comp	Eff. Rate GP	NBC
All Reps	3,189	$3,820,222	$881,820	23.1%	$25,799	0.7%	$381,931	10.0%	$356,131	40.39%	93.25%
Elders, Robert (HQ)	3,189	$3,820,222	$881,820	23.1%	$25,799	0.7%	$381,931	10.0%	$356,131	40.39%	93.25%
Conroy, Giovanni	7	$4,333	$598	13.8%	($77)	(1.8%)	($19)	(0.4%)	$57	9.60%	295.43%
Crider, Liana	128	$101,882	$32,666	32.1%	($4,741)	(4.7%)	$18,946	18.6%	$23,687	72.51%	125.02%
Dejesus, Trenton	244	$291,710	$87,150	29.9%	$12,216	4.2%	$51,380	17.6%	$39,163	44.94%	76.22%
Dickerson, Lisandra	110	$138,121	$27,951	20.2%	($16,768)	(12.1%)	$5,885	4.3%	$22,653	81.04%	384.91%
Ebert, Donovan	47	$216,476	$52,269	24.1%	$18,990	8.8%	$34,775	16.1%	$15,785	30.20%	45.39%
Farrow, Deanna	2	$606	$429	70.9%	$205	33.8%	$312	51.6%	$108	25.05%	34.42%
Fuller, Minh	324	$722,100	$190,034	26.3%	$51,490	7.1%	$125,227	17.3%	$73,737	38.80%	58.88%
Goebel, Gary	2	$491	($13)	(2.7%)	($163)	(33.1%)	($165)	(33.6%)	($3)	(19.96%)	(1.97%)
Homer, Ozella	41	$30,554	$8,138	26.6%	$1,646	5.4%	$3,735	12.2%	$2,089	25.67%	55.94%
Kiser, Shiloh	26	$340,410	$52,473	15.4%	($2,008)	(0.6%)	$26,112	7.7%	$28,121	53.59%	107.69%
Leyva, Francie	78	$82,383	$21,772	26.4%	$5,206	6.3%	$11,178	13.6%	$5,972	27.43%	53.42%
McMaster, Vonda	216	$310,011	$90,917	29.3%	$32,170	10.4%	$58,037	18.7%	$25,867	28.45%	44.57%
Nielson, Nicolette	30	$18,358	$4,998	27.2%	$530	2.9%	$1,878	10.2%	$1,348	26.97%	71.76%
Posey, Joe	1,398	$905,326	$177,238	19.6%	($72,350)	(8.0%)	($6,516)	(0.7%)	$65,834	37.14%	1,010.31%
Rogers, Fritz	90	$78,205	$18,755	24.0%	$3,420	4.4%	$8,445	10.8%	$5,025	26.79%	59.50%
Townes, Olinda	446	$579,253	$116,444	20.1%	($3,967)	(0.7%)	$42,721	7.4%	$46,688	40.09%	109.29%

figure 4.01

The other sales rep, Joe Posey, is viewed as being one of the best salespeople at the company. Joe generated about \$900,000 in revenue, \$177,000 in gross profit. However, when you look at his NBC, you realize that the company is actually \$6,500 underwater. Where the cost to serve accounts was only \$65,000 for Minh, it looks like it's something on the order of about \$180,000-185,000 for Joe Posey. Joe, who also has a base, is being paid \$65,000 on a territory that loses $6,500. That compensation only serves to compound the territory's losses, taking it from $6,500 in losses all the way up to $71,500 in losses!

For years, you may have seen your company's Joe (or Joes) as the big guy. He's the one who brings in the revenue and gets those big, fat commission checks. If you hand out awards at the end of the year, you probably have at least one Joe on that stage taking home a trophy. However, if you look back through his territory, he's been losing money for a long time. You wouldn't know that unless you took a hard look at the numbers. This is why you can't examine things by revenue. By looking at NBC, you can see that paying Joe to chase unprofitable revenue is turning a $6,500 money-losing territory into a $71,500 money-losing territory. The good news? A well-designed sales compensation plan will cut the losses in that territory by at least $65,000 and encourage Joe to only sell when it benefits the company. With Joe on the right track, that territory could become profitable.

Gross Profit vs NBC Commission

To elaborate on that idea, let's revisit that gross profit commission plan chart from the last chapter. (figure 4.02) You might recall that this chart is based on real sales information from actual companies. This particular information is based on a subset of sales transactions, along with their associated commissions, that occurred on a single day across a wide array of industries and geographies. As such, you should expect that this is happening in your business as well if your sales team is compensated on gross profit.

Under a gross profit system, a salesperson's compensation will generally shrink as the gross profit on the sales he brings in grows smaller. However, as that gross profit number approaches zero, the company stops making money on the sale (due to the added expenses of getting that product to the client) but the salesperson still receives some compensation. At a certain point, that transaction is actually underwater... but some salespeople are still making a profit!

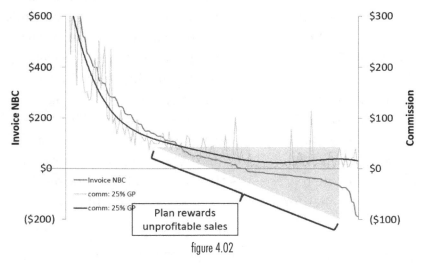

figure 4.02

The problem here is two-fold: First, you're losing money on the sale. As a general rule, you don't want sales that put the company at a loss. However, more importantly, you're providing an incentive for salespeople to bring in bad business because they're being rewarded. Subsequently you'll have salespeople either chasing unprofitable sales or making sales unprofitable by lowering the price too far.

The good news is that companies recognize these issues and many have implemented measures to prevent them. The bad news is those measures are either generally ineffective or don't work at all. A perfect example is programs that have thresholds which withhold commission if a salesperson drops below a certain amount of gross profit in a territory or on a sale. Given that the salesperson knows what that magical threshold number is, how often do you think that they'll fall below it? Instead you'll see a lot of orders which manage to make it just above that threshold (which would be great if the threshold was specifically tailored so the transaction would make money, but that's rarely the case!). The problem with thresholds, minimums, and load factors is that they're all based on gross profit or gross margin. Gross margin isn't really related to profitability. Because of things like transactional costs, it's possible to have a sale with a positive gross margin that still winds up losing you money. Especially after you pay your salesperson.

Call me old-fashioned, but I'm a firm believer that your salesperson shouldn't make money if you aren't making money. This is why you want to implement a NBC commission program since it only pays out on profitability; ie, they make money when you make money. Another important distinction is that NBC plans allow for negative commissions. If there's a sale where the company is losing money, it winds up being a deduction from the paycheck or from the commission that goes to the salesperson. This way the salespeople not only share in the profits that are generated in the territory, they also share in the losses.

Unlike the gross profit compensation system, this aligns the interests of the salesperson with that of the company. If the company has a money-losing sale which deducts from its profits elsewhere, the salesperson's negative commission causes money to be lost from his commissions made elsewhere. By sharing the loss (and subsequently reducing the company's loss on the deal), you encourage salespeople to do what's best for business.

Sales Compensation Rates

Now let's take a moment to discuss sales compensation rates. While I would wholeheartedly encourage you to use WayPoint when putting together compensation rates, there are a few alternatives that you can do as a thought exercise. I'll cover some of the ways you can calculate a rough NBC later on.

Most companies pay between 40% and 60% of the NBC to the salesperson which, I should clarify, isn't the same thing as the commission rate. Of course, there are commission plans where people are on straight commission and there are other plans that are a mix of base salary and a commission rate. In some cases, companies don't have commissions at all; they just pay a salary to their sales folks and it isn't tied to performance. However, when I look at all those numbers, regardless of what they are, industry averages usually bring companies to an endpoint where about 50-60% of the NBC that they're producing is being paid out to sales force.

I want you to check that number against your own sales force. If you don't have the NBC number through WayPoint, then you can back into it using this formula:

$$NBC = NBT + Customer\ Facing\ Rep\ Pay\ Total$$

Find the compensation rate by:

$$NBC\% = \frac{Customer\ Facing\ Rep\ Pay\ Total}{NBC} \cdot 100$$

Customer-Facing Sales Pay is the W2 gross pay amount for reps that are responsible for finding and bringing in customers.

By doing this, you find out what percentage of NBC you are paying your sales force and you can do a self-check to see where you fit. If you're paying out 20% of your NBC to the sales force then, congratulations, well done, you have an efficient and low-cost sales force. If you're paying out 80% of the NBC to the sales force, then you're behind the curve and you're paying more than you ought to. In that sort of a case, the company is a junior partner in the profit generation exercise.

Base Salary and Alternatives

When you start to look at the mechanics of a good plan, you may notice that many plans include a monthly base salary or similar base salary component. A lot of companies, even if they pay straight commission, will often wind up with such a component organically by virtue of trying to ease a salesman into the company or into starting a new territory, which I'll discuss later on.

One of the great things about having a base salary is that it smoothes out the amount of pay that goes to the sales rep. This way if the profit generation goes up or down from month to month through seasonality and other things, the fixed part of the income or the base salary compensates for the volatility and keeps the overall salary centered around a certain range.

Even if the economy goes south, and sales go down, the rep is protected because they still get their base salary regardless. The only thing that drops is the incentive part of the program. So if you look at a territory that dropped off by 10% or 15% in terms of its profit production across the course of a couple of years, what would happen is that the sales pay would only go down by half of that, it will only go down by 5% or 7.5%, and the company would wind up paying more dollars per unit profit generation across time.

The flip side is if the economy turns around and all of a sudden things are hopping along again, the company gets the benefit of the larger increase because the sales and the territory will go up by 15%. By the same token the amount of pay would only go up by half of that because only half of the pay package is variable.

Next you're probably wondering how to set those numbers, which is something that will be covered in greater detail in the next chapter. However, let's say that your company is broadly geographically based. You may have people working in downtown Manhattan while others are based in Montana. Needless to say, the cost of living is significantly different between those two places. You need around a million dollars just to buy a condo in New York, but you can get a house in Montana for a tenth of that. Subsequently the compensation needs between territories can vary wildly.

When mixing base pay with commission, you could set the same commission rate across all territories, but offer a substantially low base salary in places like Montana. The base pay component provides an easy way of tailoring compensation to each region and allows you to use the same commission rate across the company.

The two big alternatives to base pay, both of which can be seen as serving a similar function, are draws and guarantees. A guarantee is where a company says, "No matter how much you sell, I'm going to pay you at least this." The idea is that you're not going to recover it; the salesperson has a clean slate at the start of each session. This way if the rep has a really bad month, the company tops up their salary and hopefully they do better in the next month.

The problem with this system is that it doesn't necessarily encourage the salesperson to try their hardest. If salespeople see that they might not make the target that month, there's always a chance they'll just write the rest of the month off. For this reason, companies generally shy away from using guarantees. It's most commonly used for new reps, new territories, or new business segments; basically any place where you're trying to get something done and it may take a while for the salesperson to get established. A guarantee can be thought of as an investment to accomplish a goal.

By contrast, a draw against commission is when an underperforming salesman is paid extra, but that amount will be deducted from future earnings. In my experience, most draws become de facto guarantees if you have a salesperson who misses their target month after month. Eventually their compensation may be so far underwater that they're deeply in debt to the company and spiraling deeper every month. It's the ultimate de-motivator because the salesperson is so far behind that he may never see money from his commissions. It also has a serious practicality issue because not only is it difficult to recover money should the employee leave, but going after the employee with a lawsuit could seriously hurt the company's image and morale. After all, what salesperson wants to work for a company that might come after you like that?

Because management is so hesitant to recover a draw from departing employees, it effectively becomes a guarantee. Likewise, if management sees that overwhelming debt resulting from repeated draws is removing incentives to sell, they may forgive the draws and turn the policy into a guarantee.

You should be very hesitant about using draws. I can't think of even one instance across the course of my career where draws have been effective. The positives never seem to outweigh the negatives.

Tracking Compensation

The beauty of an NBC program is that it's incredibly simple. Back in the olden days, before things like WayPoint were available, distributors didn't have the tools to determine the profitability on a territory. Instead, distributors would have to bring together a lot of complex mechanics to simulate profitability or profitability indicators. This included things like gross margin rate versus the size of the sale and having different thresholds where if the territory made a certain quota then it would get a different rate. The companies would use mechanisms involving multipliers or look at KPIs to determine how somebody should perform in a territory and to see if they were exceeding their targets. These plans could wind up being enormously complex (and expensive!), both in terms of design and what was needed to track the selling activities in order to make an educated guess as to where profit was being generated.

Today, in the age of WayPoint, that number is directly known. The NBC on every invoice and territory tells distributors what costs are involved and how much money was made.

Within a good compensation program, especially in the WayPoint environment, there's going to be a certain amount of fluctuation in the numbers. For accounting purposes, the actual costs of a particular month usually aren't known within the time frame of the month. Companies have trailing invoices that come in later and some expenses get closed past the end of the billing cycle. Since it may take a while to get journal entries and other things through the system, the profitability won't immediately be known.

This has an impact on WayPoint. The most common regime in WayPoint is where the financial information is close to the end on a quarterly basis. If you look at January, you're looking at a cost structure that's finalized from the previous year on a calendar-year company and it provides a pretty good estimate of what's going on. Then, at the end of the first quarter, the books will be closed, the journal entries will be made, and the real costs become available. There may be some adjustment to the amount of profitability that I thought that I have through the projections.

In these kinds of environments, it's simple to resolve any variations. All large companies understand this and have a mechanism in place. People have been paying their management teams bonuses based on profit for as long as there have been companies and these kinds of things are usually dealt with by either delaying the bonuses until well after the end of the period or keeping them till the end of the year. However, it's a lot more effective having an incentive program that pays out at least quarterly or, in case of sales, on a monthly or periodic basis.

One way of dealing with variations is with a "true-up". At the end of January, you'll pay the salesperson based on an intelligent profit estimate and remember that payment amount. In February, you can calculate how much the person should have earned for the first two periods of the year and you will know how much has been paid out already. You'll true it up by paying out the balance. You'll essentially do that throughout the year. When you get into the commissions for the fourth period, you'll already have closed out the first quarter.

There may be some variation in how much money should have been paid. If you made more than you had projected, the rep would receive additional compensation during the true up. It may be that you've overpaid them; if you didn't make as much as you had projected, that variation will come out of the next amount paycheck. You'll wind up doing that for 12 or 13 periods throughout the year, depending on how many periods are in your calendar.

The final true up comes at the end of the year. By (or at) that point, the company will have paid the rep exactly what he was owed. This shouldn't cost a lot of dissension or problems as long as everybody understands what the rules of the game are.

Management can use discretion if the projects are wildly off for some reason. I can't recall a circumstance where this has happened with any client that I've worked with, but if it does happen, then you can take more than one period to do the true-up. You can take part of the differential out of one period and part of it the next period which gives you a mechanism for situations where you have wild variations or gyrations in the amount of pay that was calculated.

However, in WayPoint's seven or eight years, I can't recall even one instance of this happening and I wouldn't expect that to be an issue.

A good program needs a transition plan. Salespeople can't be expected to just go cold turkey when switching from one compensation program to the next. It's much better to build a plan that gives you an adequate transition period which could be anything from six months to a year.

One of the best mechanisms that I've seen was suggested by a very sharp incentive design person in New York. She helped design a program for one of our clients who was planning to start paying NBC at a certain rate. The client could see that several of their sales reps would immediately be making a lot less money because, like Joe Posey, they were either underwater or generating very low amounts of NBC.

The incentive design person suggested that, during the first quarter, the company would pay its reps the higher amount of either the new NBC program or 100% of what they had made in the same period of the year before. In the second quarter, the plan changed to where they made whatever the NBC program was or 90% of what they had made in the same period of the year before. Through the course of the year, it went from 100% down to 70% of the previous year's earnings. That gave the sales management team plenty of time to bring the reps along as they changed the nature and the mix in their territories so they had more money-making and fewer money-losing accounts.

You should always be flexible post-launch to allow for unforeseen developments. If you run into a situation where the plan is clearly not working, you need to make adjustments or course corrections. These events may be rare in a well-designed plan, but nobody can predict the future. You need to recognize and let your salespeople know that you aren't out to hurt them and adjustments can be made when the plan isn't working. Building this sort of an expectation can be very helpful in reducing any heat or smoke from an unexpected fire.

Territory Realignment

Finally, a well-designed plan should incorporate territory realignment. The goal of this process is to put your top accounts in the hands of your top reps. There's nothing worse than having a hugely profitable account disappear because that A-level account was bungled by a C-level rep. WayPoint partner Bruce Merrifield recommends that you review your sales force by putting them into two or three piles. If you look at a person and think, "Wow, this salesperson is great. Too bad I can't clone them!", then they belong in your A pile. If you look a salesperson and think, "If I could go back in time, I would have never hired this guy," then it's somebody who belongs in the C pile. All the rest go into the middle or B pile.

If you have the luxury of geographic reach or proper coverage in all the places where you need sales, you could have your best accounts in the hands of your best reps. You can re-balance the territories so they have a good mix of money-making and money-losing accounts, so your most able salespeople will have an opportunity to turn money-losing accounts profitable.

The A reps would spend an increased amount of time on a numerically smaller territory made up of larger accounts where they can really shine and add new large accounts to the territory. The people that are better with mid-range accounts could specialize in the mid-range accounts. In short, having the right people working on the right kinds of accounts can give you a tremendous advantage. As you work through the territory alignment, you may find that some of your C reps aren't really needed at all. You can look at reducing the sales force by getting rid of some of the C reps who may be creating a drag on sales and the overall profit performance of the company.

To quickly recap, the goal of a well-designed sales compensation program is to bring compensation levels in line with profit production. A sales person should only make money when you do. A base salary can provide performance insurance and help to smooth out sales compensation. I also discussed a few of the ways you make sure that sales pay is driven by profit and still delivered in a timely manner. I hope you also learned a little more about setting up a transition plan and the value of territory reassignment. With that out of the way, the next chapter will delve into some of the hard numbers.

Managing Money-Losing Accounts

A profit-driven compensation plan generally reduces the requirement for the close management normally exercised in a sales force. This is generally because close management is required when the incentive plan encourages results not good for the business. (i.e. encouraging money-losing sales while paying commissions on such sales)

A major exception for a profit-driven plan is where the sales rep can drive off potentially-profitable money-losing accounts rather than working to make them profitable. This is problematic because such an activity foregoes the longer-term opportunities those accounts represent.

Management much be on top of this risk, and actively manage with the possibility in mind.

Transition Plans

From the time first asked, reps will need time to work with customers to change the Gross Profit to Cost-to-Serve ratio that drive profit and sales pay. If you're unable to aggressively change your sales force structure to bring it in line with profit production, you'll need to create mechanisms to take pay / profit performance from current levels to the desired end state over a period of time.

Most transition plans run from six to twelve months.

Recognizing that each existing territory may have much more or much less distance from the desired end-state, it's logical that a single parameter may not suit every territory. You'll get a lot of freedom by using a flexible plan to get everyone to the end state at their own speed (within limits).

One excellent transition plan that I've seen used works by paying either amounts based on historic performance or the new rate, whichever is most favorable to the rep. However, the historic component diminishes over time.

Specifically, the transition might be stated this way: for the first quarter, the rep will get the greater of either the new plan amount or what was paid in the same period last year.

For the second quarter, the greater of the new plan or 90% of last year. In the third, the greater of the new plan or 80% of last year, followed by 70% in the fourth. After that, only the new plan applies.

This gives the reps time to work on profit issues with their accounts, while making it impossible for those that won't to maintain high pay levels on under-performing territories.

You may invent or adopt other mechanisms that achieve the same goals.

Designing a Plan

Previous chapters have discussed what a successful sales compensation plan should cover and gone into some of the mechanics that enable those things. This chapter will delve into the numbers that go into the actual plan and will hopefully help you figure out some calculations for commission rates.

To quickly recap lessons from previous chapters, a NBC Commission Plan will meet the following parameters:

- ✓ It will pay incentives on a territory or customer NBC—that means that costs are going to be taken into account and it's going to pay for actual profitability.
- ✓ It will eliminate incentives for dysfunctional sales— that means it will withdraw commissions or have negative commissions for negative profit sales.
- ✓ It will reward efforts to reform unprofitable business—that means higher pay for people who are working to make the company more profitable by turning unprofitable accounts into profitable accounts.
- ✓ It will synchronize the goals of the company and the goals of the sales force.
- ✓ It will reduce or eliminate the adversarial component present in most sales regimes, where salespeople are paid to bring in dysfunctional or negative profit

business after which sales managers being paid to stop them from doing it.

✓ It will be much easier to implement and administer. The calculations of sales become very simple and allow you to look directly at profitability rather than using other factors to simulate what may be adversely or positively impacting profitability.

In short, a NBC Plan is the most effective technique for rapidly increasing profitability. It gets the sales force working on the profit issues and, because a large portion of the potential profit gains are on the customer contact's surface of the business, this greatly improves the company's overall profitability. A truly great sales force won't just help your customer become more profitable but it will find new ways to help your customers expand their business as well.

Set Baseline Values and Test

The first step in putting together your commission calculations involves setting some baseline values. The purpose of the baseline is to make sure that the numbers that you intend to use as the factors for commission rates, for base salaries, and for the other components of the plan are realistic and thus will work. You can establish your baseline by taking the NBC production for each of the reps, preferably from the previous year, then map it with the total take-home pay (commission and/or salary) for those reps from the previous year. This should give you the effective pay-out rate.

Now it's time to balance the system. Since you probably haven't been paying on profitability in the past, you want to determine which reps are being overpaid for profits that they bring in and which ones are being underpaid. You will likely discover a lot dysfunction within your current pay system. Those issues will be straightened out as you use territory realignments, adjust base salaries (or NBC rates), and use guarantees to set a pay scheme up that should pay the right amount of money in every possible circumstance.

You will then back-test against prior performance. WayPoint has an easy and intuitive way of doing that, but in the world of high-end compensation design, companies don't always have the budget to do back-testing since it could add another $50,000 to $250,000 in additional expenses on a project. Companies that don't back-test risk having certain issues because it will be more difficult to account for every circumstance or spot the anomalies that inevitably exist in the sales flow (and can have an adverse effect on pay!). However, you won't have to worry about that since I'm going to walk you through some testing methods.

NBC Compensation Sheet

The first thing that I'm going to take a look at is the NBC compensation worksheet. This is just a rough sample to help illustrate the concepts.

There are three blocks in a NBC worksheet: the top block shows the previous payouts under the old system, the second block allows us to play with base salaries, and the third box allows us to play with commission rates to work out what those numbers should be from those different perspectives.

Each column represents a particular performance level typical of reps in different categories. I recommend, whenever possible, to put every rep into the program since it should reveal all of the different performance levels and pay levels. It's best to take this information down to a monthly level so that you can see what outliers exist throughout the year and make sure that your plan properly accommodates them.

I should start by warning you that no one mathematical rate will apply to all people in all circumstances. You can spend a great deal of time trying to find a magical set of numbers, commission rates, and base salaries that work under all circumstances, but it's almost always an exercise in futility. You aren't on a search for a perfect set of numbers that will meet all conditions; instead you're looking for a good set of numbers that will meet most conditions and then make sure that you have enough flexibility to accommodate the outliers. A successful plan will change when you run into unplanned circumstances or a shift in the environment.

History	A	B	C	D
FY NBC	$190,000	$120,000	$200,000	$200,000
FY W2	$63,000	$58,000	$63,000	$63,000
NBC rate	33.2%	48.3%	31.5%	31.5%
fixed base	$55,000	$45,000	$55,000	$55,000
incent	$8,000	$13,000	$8,000	$8,000
total pay	$63,000	$58,000	$63,000	$63,000
NBC rate	4.2%	10.8%	4.0%	4.0%
fixed rate	10%	10%	10%	10%
adj base	$44,000	$46,000	$43,000	$43,000
incent	$19,000	$12,000	$20,000	$20,000
total pay	$63,000	$58,000	$63,000	$63,000

figure 5.01

The first row in the first block of numbers contains the NBC that was produced by the reps in the previous year. The second row has the actual W-2 pay. This excludes things like benefits, since those things apply to wide swaths of the company. Trying to factor them in just adds unnecessary complexity and makes it that much harder to communicate the plan to sales reps. Above all, you should be talking to salespeople in the same vernacular that they're accustomed to hearing what their base pay is and what they're going to see on their check.

The performance information from the first block tells us that in the first case that the company effectively paid out 33.2% of all the NBC that was made for the rep in Case A, 48.3% for the rep in Case B.

The next part of the plan is where you plug in a fixed base salary. This will show what incentives need to be paid in order to bring the pay up to last year's W-2 and what sort of a NBC rate is needed to accommodate the fixed base. If you have a $55,000 base rate, you would need a 4.2% NBC rate to arrive at the same result. The $45,000 base salary would wind up with a 10.8% NBC rate. As you may have already realized, you would need different NBC rates in order to accommodate the fixed bases for these reps.

While it's okay to pay different rates for different people, that could get unmanageable as your sales force gets broader and may leave opportunities for people to twiddle numbers somewhere that won't be noticed. I wouldn't recommend that you come up with individual rates for each person, but it's a useful exercise to find out what the rates might be. Just going by the first two here, it looks like a 7.5% rate would split the difference. This provides us with a starting point.

The third block is where you get to plug in a NBC rate and it will tell you what base salary is needed to accommodate that particular rate. What's interesting is that you can just take 10% as a round number and you would get an adjusted base rate of $44,000 for one salesperson and $46,000 for the other to wind up with the same pay for the same results. By adjusting the rate upward and the base salary downward to synchronize them more closely, you wind up with a single rate that would apply fairly well in both territories. That can provide some indication of where to go forward.

Now it's time to switch to the actual, live spreadsheet. Listed here are the reps from a particular branch. The information includes their names, their NBC from last year, the W-2 from last year, and the NBC rate. This spreadsheet provides a fairly typical view of the mathematics that go on when you're coming from a pay scheme based on gross margin or gross profit instead of profitability. These numbers should give you some idea of the real dysfunction in that can occur in those older systems.

	A	B	C	D	E	F
1						
2	History	A	B	C	D	D
3		Coggins	Anders	Daley	Dotson	Frederick
4	FY NBC	($95,641)	$272,540	$12,892	$7,391	($12,860)
5	FY W2	$135,658	$121,275	$33,145	$10,812	$4,488
6	NBC rate	-141.8%	44.5%	257.1%	146.3%	-34.9%
7						
8	fixed base	$50,000	$50,000	$50,000	$50,000	$50,000
9	incent	$85,658	$71,275	($16,855)	($39,188)	($45,512)
10	total pay	$135,658	$121,275	$33,145	$10,812	$4,488
11	NBC rate	-89.6%	26.2%	-130.7%	-530.2%	353.9%
12						
13	fixed rate	10%	10%	10%	10%	10%
14	adj base	$145,222	$94,021	$31,856	$10,073	$5,774
15	incent	($9,564)	$27,254	$1,289	$739	($1,286)
16	total pay	$135,658	$121,275	$33,145	$10,812	$4,488
17						

figure 5.02

Case in point is a rep (Frederick) who was generating a negative NBC while getting paid very well. It's a rate that's completely unworkable. (figure 5.02) Since there are no indicators for how it could be turned profitable, it would take some extra legwork to come up with the right numbers.

Let's take a look at Anders in the B Column. Anders generated $272,000 NBC and that produced $121,000 in pay. The sheet shows me that I need to have about a 44% NBC rate in order to maintain that kind of pay level. I can plug in various base rates and come out with various commission rates. If the guy is on a $4,000/month base salary, that would be $48,000 a year, then I can plug that in and see that I need about a 27% rate for him.

Britney Salerno is also somewhat in the ballpark. It makes sense to look at the most reasonable accounts first, like Salerno, to get a baseline for the kind of performance I want. Right now she's getting $68,000 for $131,000 of performance; that's about a 52% rate. If I wanted to have her make last year's pay then I might give her around a $3,000/month base, which is $36,000, then I've got a 24.7% rate. When I compare the 26.9% from Anders against the 24.7% from Salerno, it looks like something in the 25.5-26% might be an appropriate pay level. If I want to pay a 25% base rate, I can give $53,000 base to Anders, $35,000 base for Salerno, and this gives me an idea of where the pay needs to be in order to accommodate this.

Looking back at the rep list, you'll notice some areas where the numbers are completely dysfunctional. These are places where the territory is underwater, but the rep is still being paid and other places where the rep requires more than all the profit in the territory just to make their living. There are two things you should take away from information.

The first takeaway is that it reveals a dysfunction in normal gross profit pay processes, where I'm actually paying good salaries for people to bring us no or negative profitability. This one of the things that you want to fix and the reason you're changing your compensation program.

The second takeaway is that the territories themselves are probably composed of an inappropriate balance or combination of customers which may be driving things so far negative. Territory realignments are the key to getting a set of numbers that's going to be functional, so part of what you may wind up doing is rebuilding or realigning the territories at the NBCs for newly aligned territories and plugging them into this model so that you have someplace that you can go.

Above all, it's important to remember that the territories haven't been managed on an NBC or profitability basis. Anything that has never been managed will see enormous improvement by having a little bit of attention paid to something that affects the profitability. For that reason, keep in mind that the salespeople have the ability to change the territories pretty substantially in short order. As such, the amount of compensation that I'm planning on paying using this model may wind up being increased pretty substantially as the salespeople start to affect the profitability of the customers in the territory. This shouldn't be a cause for concern because a good NBC program will always pay out of profit that you gain. Since the profits grow at the same time that the payouts increase, the company won't be underwater through pay increases.

Territory Reassignment

The purpose of the territory reassignment is to build territories that are functional for each of the reps. When

WayPoint partner Bruce Merrifield does it at its most ruthless level, you may recall that he'll do it through an exercise of categorizing the sales reps. All of the top guys go in the A pile while all of the worst salespeople wind up in the C pile. Everyone in-between winds up in B.

Bruce may start by taking an accumulated profit report, ranked on NBC, out of WayPoint. He will recognize that he needs, for instance, $200,000 or $400,000 of NBC to pay his top guy. If there are no geographic issues and everything is in one place or within the territory, then you can work on giving the sales rep enough accounts to get him to that amount.

	Customer	Revenue		GP		NBC	
		$	Accum	$	Accum	$	Accum
1	I Party Retail Store	1,040,103	1,040,103	12.0%	122,682	122,682	7.1%	76,402	76,402	12.6%
2	12th Street Ht Associat...	863,280	1,903,383	22.0%	119,337	242,020	14.1%	71,982	148,383	24.5%
3	Uniland Partnership of...	412,012	2,315,395	26.8%	61,835	303,855	17.7%	46,520	194,903	32.2%
4	Kilian Mfg Co	180,164	2,495,559	28.9%	50,752	354,607	20.6%	37,829	232,732	38.5%
5	Premier Seating Comp...	207,863	2,703,422	31.3%	59,261	413,868	24.0%	32,345	265,077	43.8%
6	Disc Graphics Inc	254,517	2,957,939	34.2%	56,961	470,829	27.4%	31,375	296,452	49.0%
7	Columbia Communicat...	226,799	3,184,738	36.8%	33,655	504,484	29.3%	29,315	325,767	53.9%
8	Dynamics Research C...	321,999	3,506,738	40.6%	48,499	552,983	32.1%	28,879	354,646	58.6%
9	Kelley Steel Erectors Inc	231,400	3,738,137	43.2%	54,974	607,957	35.3%	24,970	379,616	62.8%
10	Equitrans L P	173,538	3,911,676	45.2%	36,860	644,817	37.5%	24,236	403,852	66.8%
11	Medical Life Insurance...	160,121	4,071,796	47.1%	57,275	702,092	40.8%	23,668	427,520	70.7%
12	Westover Companies	246,702	4,318,498	50.0%	49,865	751,957	43.7%	10,010	437,530	72.3%
13	Choate Hall & Stewart	157,440	4,475,939	51.8%	46,047	798,004	46.4%	9,983	447,512	74.0%
14	David Penske Chevrol...	244,558	4,720,497	54.6%	59,598	857,602	49.8%	9,685	457,198	75.6%
15	Interdigital Communica	81,095	4,801,592	55.5%	13,555	871,157	50.6%	9,239	466,437	77.1%

figure 5.03

In this scenario, the first ten accounts get us to $403,852. There could be a salesperson that had 130 accounts and wasn't getting to most of them, but now he can focus in on enough accounts to give him the kind of pay he needs. This way he can spend more time working on those accounts which will allow him to penetrate them more deeply, finding more things that they can buy and improved ways of integrating with the customers to make it more profitable for both parties.

You may also consider adding some negative accounts into the mix (I'll explain the benefits a little later on), but the important thing is that you wind up with a finite number of accounts that belong in that territory. Then you might decide that you need $300,000 of territory for the next guy.

As you repeat this process, you'll eventually start to run out of accounts that make money. At that point you'll probably wonder, what are these other guys going to do? Do they wind up being transferred into more of a tele-sales role where they're working on smaller customers on a more remote basis and not driving out in cars, knocking on doors? Do they serve other purposes? Or do they just not need to be there?

The scope of what I'm talking about isn't about how to rearrange the sales force with the intention of letting people go, but ultimately you're going to wind up having a certain amount of NBC that has to generate enough income for your salespeople. If you have a branch where the whole sales force is underwater, what the numbers are really telling you is you have too much money going out for the profit you receive. How do you fix that? Part of the solution is obviously have less money go out on accounts that are either losing or not making money.

A little earlier I discussed handing out a certain number of money-losing accounts. In the case of the A salesperson from earlier, his new territory might also include the five biggest money-losing accounts. You could add a few more accounts from the top to keep him at $400,000 total, but he'd also have some negative accounts that he could work to turn profitable. Doing so offers a few benefits.

The first thing benefit is that it gives the salesperson some room to grow. He can do some things that increase the profitability of the business and increase his own income at the same time, which can help to build enthusiasm. If you have your top guy, who likely is also the sales force's opinion leader, praising the new program and discussing how it's led him to be more successful, then others may be inspired to follow his example. This will encourage them to make the plan work for themselves and focus on driving profitability.

The second benefit is that now you have somebody working to fix your negative accounts. These kinds of accounts may have been neglected or improperly handled. They could have substantial profitability lying right below the surface but the previous salesperson handling the account may not have had the ability to get at the profit. However, if you have your top guys working on the accounts, you may see improvements fairly quickly. And, since these accounts may have been very unprofitable, you should see a substantial profitability shift.

NBC Commission Report

Let's take a look at the NBC Commission Report generated by the WayPoint Sales Compensation Calculator. This particular report is interesting because it allows for negative commissions. In the case of Olinda Townes, she had positive NBC on some accounts and negative NBC on others. She had a total of $2,000 NBC for the period and she wound up with $1,000 worth of commission. She made almost $1,000 of commission on her best account, another $200 on her second best, but she lost $176 of commission on her worst account which was underwater in terms of NBC.

The report has a few interesting applications. This report actually gets printed out and is included with the paycheck.

It tells the HR people what they should pay the sales rep and explains to the salesperson the reason for their earnings. In this case, the total commission was $1,021. If she had no money-losing accounts then she would have made $1360. If all of her accounts were running at the average NBC rate of her profitable accounts, she would have made almost $1,800. In all, she could have made 80% more in this month if she had worked on her underperforming accounts and brought them up at least just to the average of her money-making accounts.

400 Anders, Fred								Date: 3/15/2010 Fiscal Period: 201002
Customer	Orders	(NBC)	Rev	GP	GM%	NBC	NBC%	Comm
6981 Interdigital Communications Corporation	1	0%	$78,077	$12,375	15.8%	$10,596	13.6%	$3,708.53
1445 Kilian Mfg Co	14	14%	$25,531	$7,959	31.2%	$6,104	23.9%	$2,136.26
2922 Dynamics Research Corporation	8	38%	$28,057	$5,210	18.6%	$3,932	14.0%	$1,376.34
3489 Disc Graphics Inc	11	0%	$19,681	$4,885	24.8%	$2,627	13.3%	$919.28
6349 12th Street Ht Associatates LP	28	55%	$83,226	$7,853	9.4%	$1,943	2.3%	$680.19
343 Hyde Park Savings Bank	2	0%	$5,761	$1,512	26.2%	$1,089	18.9%	$381.07
4989 Cleveland Energy Resources	1	0%	$1,595	$666	41.8%	$448	28.1%	$156.86
1468 Uniland Partnership of Del LP	1	0%	$1,605	$419	26.1%	$251	15.6%	$87.80
392 New America High Income Fund	1	0%	$1,696	$460	27.1%	$190	11.2%	$66.62
1007 Great Lakes Lithograph Co	1	100%	$234	$64	27.3%	($42)	-18.0%	($14.70)
5262 Tweeter Home Entertainment Group Inc	1	100%	$817	$115	14.1%	($91)	-11.2%	($31.92)
683 Equitrans L P	5	40%	($3,663)	$215	-5.9%	($518)	14.2%	($181.45)
563 First American Equity Ln Svcs	13	86%	$5,791	$1,296	22.4%	($1,301)	-22.5%	($455.30)
			$248,409	$43,031		$25,227		$8,829.59

Customers: 13
Orders: 87
Invoices: 90
Money-Losing Invoices: 41.1%

Gross Margin: 17%
NBC Rate: 10%

Total Commissions: $8,829.59
(if you had no money-losing sales): $11,158.99
(if all sales were at your average profit rate): $11,692.79

Base Pay: $2,000.00
Commissions: $8,829.59
Other Pay: $0.00
Adjustments: $0.00
Total Pay: $10,829.59

figure 5.04

This gives a clear indicator of how much money is available. On a monthly basis, it reminds salespeople what they should be doing, what they shouldn't be doing, which accounts are helping with their commissions, and which accounts are harming their commissions. This can help them identify exactly what they should be working on.

Benefits of an NBC Plan

To recap some of the new lessons learned in this chapter, a NBC Plan will:

- ✓ Motivate the top reps because the best reps are going to have above average earnings. This is especially true when you launch the plan and start managing the previously unmanaged aspects of profitability in the accounts. This usually means big gains in profitability which, in turn, means big gains in income for the reps. Since that increased income is fully funded by the profitability increase, the company's budget stays under control.
- ✓ Promote high morale because it makes sure that top performers get rewarded while underperformers make far less. This sends a message to the sales force that the company cares whether people perform or underperform. It lets the reps know that they are really masters of their own success, in terms of being able to choose what they work on and how they work on it.
- ✓ Finally the low performers will be low-paid which may lead them to fire themselves, thus saving you from having to swing the ax. Sales can be a tough racket and not everybody is cut out for the work. This could free them up to find something better suited to their talents. Best of all? You won't good accounts in the hands of bumbling reps.

In the next chapter, you'll learn how launch your new plan, how to put together communication elements, and what kinds of things you have to be aware of post-launch in order for the plan to be successful.

Launching Your Plan

So far I've discussed the benefits of a sales compensation plan, the elements that go into its design, and the numbers that make it work. Now you've reached to the really exciting part: Launching the plan.

The launch phase of the plan may be the most critical section. Whether your plan sinks or swims can depend entirely on its implementation. There have been countless plans invented by terrifically intelligent people that have absolutely tanked during their roll-out because the launch phase wasn't planned out with the same care and detail that went into the rest of the plan mechanics. This is why I can't stress enough that you need to a great job on launch.

Here are the six most important points that I'll discuss in this chapter. If your launch plan manages to hit all six, you should be in excellent shape.
1) You want to plan in private but not in secret.
2) You want to use or develop flexible rules for the plan (because it's impossible to anticipate everything!).
3) You want to plan crediting rules so salespeople will know what is or isn't included in the plan.
4) You want to use true-ups, which help to compensate for an inability to track profits in real time.

5) You want to have a transition component to help remove anxieties and ease salespeople from the old system to the new one.

6) You want to communicate intelligently and set proper expectations so that your sales team will really consider how the plan may benefit them.

Plan in Private (But Not in Secret)

It's almost impossible in most organizations to spend weeks (or even months) putting together a new compensation plan without anybody finding out. When that planning process is uncovered, the sales force will automatically suspect that the plan intends to make company more profitable at their expense by reducing their commissions. Left to their own devices, the rumors start flying and the salespeople will be ready to protest your plan before they even see it.

I recommend that you plan in private so that you can have the space to consider alternatives which may be unpopular. You might not use these alternatives, but at least you'll go through them without getting people riled up. You don't want your salespeople to see this side of the process but, at the same time, you don't want to make your sales team suspicious.

You can handle this by letting the sales force know that you're taking a look at plan alternatives because you believe there may be a better way of rewarding people for pursuing the things that matter most to the company. You could say something like, "I'm looking to make another million dollars next year and I want to find a way to share some of those profits with you." This could capture your sales team's curiosity and hopefully get them looking forward to your plan being unveiled. Whatever you tell them, make sure that it helps your salespeople understand that the plan will ultimately benefit them as well.

You'll probably have at least a few salespeople who hate change and some of them might enjoy causing trouble by getting everybody riled up. It's important to identify those people early on so you can sit down with them and explain that this sort of behavior isn't appreciated. You should keep your ear to the ground at all times so you can respond quickly when rumors crop up. If these rumors start to get disruptive, you can call a meeting to straighten a few things out or give your team some idea as to the current progress.

One of the best things that you can do in these kinds of discussion is say, "I'm looking at plan alternatives that work well with our numbers and with each salesperson's numbers. I want to make sure I come up with the right amount of pay for everybody and those helping us move the ball down the field should expect better pay."

You can tell them that you've done Phases 1 and 2, you're working on 3, and 4 is still to come. Just give them some information about what's going on, but be a little vague and general about it. If they'll press you for specifics, you can respond, "Things are in a state of flux and changing every day as I discover things that I want to fine-tune. I'm just going to hold off going into detail until I have it complete plan where everything is worked out." The sales force should feel that they're being informed and have some idea of what to expect, because it will affect them.

It's important to identify your team's opinion leaders and make sure that they're on board. I've all been in meetings where, when somebody says something, all heads turn to the one salesperson whose opinion they're waiting for. When that person speaks, everybody seems to agree. You want these kinds of people to have some involvement in the planning process; you could even make them part of the planning committee. If you don't want to do that, you may bring them right before your plan launches and ask for their opinions on the plan. Give them an opportunity to suggest some tweaks which can give them a sense of ownership of the plan. This way when the plan comes out and all heads turn to them, they're nodding yes.

Be aware that this isn't always possible. There are certain kinds of people who are difficult to get on board which can pose a challenge if one such person is in a thought leadership role. However, for the most part, the more successful senior salespeople usually have the company's best interests in heart and can be counted on to use their leadership role to help the company advance its objective.

Use Flexible Rules

When's the last time anything in your life has gone exactly as you had foreseen? For most people, the answer is almost never. There are too many unforeseen variables at work at any given moment to anticipate every possibility, which is why it's important that your plan have flexible rules.

As a numbers guy, I have a great deal of empathy for other numbers guys who like having square corners on the boxes and everything inside the circle. Unfortunately, the world's a messy place and there will always be something that doesn't work properly. Whether it's something that only management notices or the whole team is in on it, the question becomes what are you going to do about it?

The worst decision is sticking exactly to the plan when there's an obvious problem. However, you could run into issues with middle management where those individual might recognize an issue but don't feel that they have the authority to make a change. For this reason, it's important work with middle managers to make sure that you have a feedback mechanism in payroll, HR, or other places so the company can be made aware of and work to resolve any legitimate issues.

I want you to keep the following things in mind:

✓ Avoid rigid mathematics, especially when it comes to things like credit rules. If you must, you can change the actual metrics in the plan to work on something that better suits the current environment. However, this should be sparingly because you don't want to have a situation where somebody might get bullied into modifying almost every part of the plan until it's no longer able to function financially.

✓ Account for outliers. There may be circumstances where somebody is handling a territory and it goes to zero for some uncontrollable reason. Keep an eye out for those kinds of things and try to learn from them whenever possible. Most companies can tolerate a little unexpected variance, but too much variation going in the same direction can prove problematic.

✓ Prepare for course corrections. Watch how the plan performs each quarter during the first year so you can spot and correct anything that might have gone wrong. Announcing this kind of a plan up front will let your sales team know that you're going to be responsive to what's going on.

✓ Schedule it. Even the best of plans will require a certain amount of fine-tuning. Scheduling those changes in can help to make the plan more sustainable and lead to something which will provide great benefits for the company and its employees for years to come.

Plan Crediting Rules

Crediting rules are often overlooked in plan design, much to the detriment of the plan's designers. Crediting rules essentially dictate what qualifies (or doesn't qualify) for incentives and how those incentives are timed. It may say things like, "I pay on this but I do not pay commissions on service," and, "I pay commissions on new sales at a different rate than I do on old sales."

These rules explain how to translate an invoice amount into an incentive amount. When putting together your rules, you need to consider the breadth of the product line and the service envelope for your customer, how commissions are going to be triggered, and the timing of the commission payments.

These things need to be clearly articulated so that the people who work payroll will calculate the payroll period. Unless you use a system like the WayPoint Analytics System for commissions, your payroll people will need to know the rules so they can reach the correct numbers and issue those payments within the correct time frame.

Most of this seems obvious, but all too often something winds up overlooked. This is the first and most common place for a plan to start to have holes. Only proper planning and communication can avoid some pretty serious errors.

Use True-Ups

Most profitability plans have a time-facing issue. As you're no doubt well aware, it's difficult to know everything that happened in a particular period, quarter, or even year since there are a lot of things that affect the financials. Most companies take about three weeks to close a period (and closing a quarter or year will take even longer) due to the various follow-ups involved in the invoicing process, with vendors, and so on.

For that reason, profit-based plans will rarely have all of the information available when the commissions are being calculated. Companies within the universal WayPoint plan that close a period, if they're on a calendar month, will often close the period at the end of March, but they won't actually get the books closed for about three weeks.

In many cases, the commissions for the period are due in the middle of the following period, which would only give 15 days to do the calculations and get them into the payroll system. However, the payroll service you use may only have 10 days to get things done. In the worst case scenario, there may be two weekends in that 10-day period which could reduce that window even further.

You also should consider that some companies don't close all their billings on the last day of the month; there may be a two-day window to close the billings out. So in the absolute worst case scenario, the payroll people may only have two days of working time before the payroll has to be calculated so that it can go out. In these scenarios, you would have to use estimates.

In the WayPoint case, I won't know what the financials are until the end of the period at best, and even then they still have to be processed in the system. To compensate for this, WayPoint always uses the last known metrics for how the costs are structured in the company until it gets the updates from the finance team.

On the first of January, WayPoint will use the numbers from the previous year to calculate costs and profitability. It continues to do that for all of January until the end of the month when I can put the January numbers in then restate the calculations. The same thing will happen each period and quarter. I may not have financial information until the end of the first quarter, so it might be late April before the real numbers become available for March. Three pay cycles may have ended (putting us in the fourth cycle) before WayPoint really knows what the real profits were.

How do you deal with that? The answer is that, in high-end designs, you would use a process called a true-up. Here's how it works: At the end of January, when WayPoint will tell you what it thinks the commissions were, you pay an amount based on the estimated profitability. At the end of February, the same thing will accrue. At the end of March, the same thing will accrue.

In April, you'll get the real numbers. At that point you calculate everything that should have been paid for the first four periods then deduct from that the amount of pay that was already paid. Finally, you would pay out the balance. If the rep has been underpaid, then the company will make good on that by saying, "Well, our profits were better than expected so I'm able to pay you a bit more." Conversely, if the rep had been overpaid, the company will say, "I pre-paid some of the money that you hadn't yet earned, but here's the rest."

If there's too much fluctuation, you might consider adding some mechanisms to the true-up. If somebody looks to be making a lot of money but it turns out the profitability has been zero, you can't just tell the person to suck it up. You would need to do something, however, which is where the flexible rules come in.

The purpose of true-ups is to make sure that things are synchronized at the end of each quarter, financial period, and year so that the amount of money paid matches the amount earned. Of course, there are other ways of making sure that compensation is matched against profit generation. I've known companies with programs that are similar in terms of the payouts having draws against commission or a similar function. These are fairly common in sales and they won't cause any issues, assuming that you're clear in your communication and set good expectations. If people go into the system cold because you forgot to say something or didn't make things perfectly clear, then you risk having a pretty sizable problem on your hands.

Have a Transition Component

As I discussed in the last chapter, a transition component is a way of easing your sales team from the old system to the new one. Most transition plants last at least six months and some might be in place for a year. The best transition mechanics give salespeople the opportunity to change how they do with business with their customers so that profits can be generated more effectively. This is something that will take time. On the first day, customers are naturally going to be doing the same dysfunctional things they were on the day before. Just like your sales force, customers need to be eased into your new way of doing business.

You may remember my story in a previous chapter about that really smart consultant from Rochester, NY, who suggested a transition plan that would gradually scale down. For the first quarter, the sales reps get the higher amount of either whatever the new plan paid or what they made the same quarter last year. In the second quarter, they would get 90% of whatever the new plan pays or 90% of what they earned last year. In the third quarter it went to 80%, in the fourth quarter it went to 70%, and after that they were on the new plan.

This strategy helped one our clients smoothly transition into a massively successful new plan. This company actually went from losing money to becoming a solid, profitable company for the past five consecutive years. This company isn't just generating industry-leading profitability but it actually increased its revenue since the beginning of the recession by 40% despite only having around 60% of its original customers.

How did the client do it? The company pursued its plan aggressively, getting the sales people through the transition while finding outstanding replacements for the few salespeople who weren't ready to get on board. The reps made substantially more and now there's a gain-sharing bonus for the entire company. Last year, that gain-sharing bonus was $6,700 per employee which came from the $76,000 profit gain per employee over the year before. The new plan dramatically improved the take-home for both the company and its employees. It was a perfect win-win.

My advice to you is to stick to the plan. There will always be somebody who will gripe about the new plan and want to return to the old one. If you've carefully designed your plan, you have no reason to back down. Of course, if you made a mess with the plan and everybody is in complete disaster mode, then it is your fault and you will have to go back to the drawing board. If you have one or two squeaky wheels, then you have to figure out what you're going to do about that, but you should stay with the plan because if you get to the end point, it pays.

Communicate Intelligently

Rates, calculations, crediting rules, timing, and transition all need to be thoroughly documented. When I worked at a specialized sales compensation firm, our delivery paperwork would include a complete document that outlined the entire plan. Each sales rep sign would have to sign a copy of the document which then went into the record. This works as an acknowledgment that the reps both understand and agree to the new compensation rules. While this is especially important in some jurisdictions, it's a good idea for everybody.

The other part of intelligent communication goes back to acknowledging and dealing with rumors. The same rumor mill that can pop up during the planning process will still be there when your plan is getting underway. However, now you have concrete details to squash any rumors. Make sure that you communicate your plan and objectives thoroughly, answering questions when you can and referring people to the written documentation. Above all, you want your salespeople to understand that the company wants to make more money and share that money more efficiently with the salespeople who contribute the most to the company's bottom line.

Common Failure Modes

Common failure modes include not planning for outliers and having many exceptions because you either didn't recognize or didn't build them into your crediting rules or plan mechanics. When you don't test for each salesperson, then you risk somebody coming in with less than half of their expected pay or possibly 500% of their expected pay. These outliers make for very difficult situations and are something you want to have worked out in the plan mechanics beforehand.

Another common issue is failing to set proper expectations. Your team needs to believe that this system doesn't just benefit the company, but it will help them as well. Your salespeople should understand that nothing is set in stone; if something absolutely doesn't work, there will be a change. You may want to communicate something along the lines of, "I'm doing the best I can. I'm working hard on a great system, but there will always be some oversights for us to correct. Just be assured that I'm working diligently to make the company more profitable so you can get paid more for your contributions."

The one thing you can't do is chicken out. There may be challenges within your new plan. Remember that anything worth doing will have challenges. If you're going to implement a profit-based plan successfully, you need to make a commitment and then stick to it. You don't want to buckle when, at the first sign of trouble, your sales people insist that the plan has failed and want you to go back to the old compensation model.

The leading cause of failure is quitting. Business leaders will begin to implement their plan, but they just don't have the guts to get to the next level. It's unfortunate because, as business leaders, I always like to think I'm managing the business rather than letting the business manage us. However, sometimes the reverse is true and, in that kind of an environment, it's almost impossible to meet increased standards or objectives. A management team will never be successful if you can't get hard things done.

Start Creating Your Plan Today

When is the perfect time to take control of your company's profitability with a profit-based compensation plan? Is it within the next period? ...the next quarter? ...the next year? I want you to ask yourself a hard question: If you don't make the commitment today, will you ever start working on a profit-based sales compensation plan?

Because transition periods can take six to twelve months, being on a profit-driven plan for next fiscal year will require you start the process *now*. Getting the sales force on a plan that synchronizes their goals with the company's can be a powerful device to move profit performance beyond all records. *Now is the last opportunity to change the profit performance of this month and this year.*

Having this book, you now have the tools and the knowledge at your disposal to begin crafting your own profit-based sales compensation plan. What will you do with this knowledge? The power is in your hands.

I want to tell you about one of the best companies in our entire WayPoint universe. This company has a sales force where the lowest paid rep makes over a quarter million dollars a year. The highest paid rep makes about three-quarter million a year. This company has been paying on profits for a very long time and, as a result, is an absolute cash cow despite being one of the most difficult commoditized businesses in a very crowded, very competitive market. The client stuck to its guns, it made the transition, and it has experienced tremendous rewards for the effort.

Another, much smaller WayPoint client company adopted this kind of plan, helping the reps (and the company) focus exclusively on the most profitable customers. The result: average pay increase of $30,000 for the reps, and a company bottom line *more than five times any previous year!*

I want to encourage you to consider getting a plan going within your own company immediately. A profit-based sales compensation plan is one of the most valuable tools you can use to drive profitability and gains in profits in your business. It doesn't come without a cost, anything worthwhile requires some effort, but if you're willing to make the changes and follow the guidelines in this book, it is almost impossible for one of these plans to fail. If you implement the plan properly, your company experience dramatically improved profitability.

I sincerely hope that the information I've provided will help you map out your own plan and I wish all the best as you go about unlocking your company's true potential and profitability.

Plan Design Walk-Through

From this point, I'll walk through the details of creating a design in detail. I'll work out a design for a fictitious smaller distributor I'll call "Acme Distributing"—the company that supplies Wile E Coyote with the materials he uses to attempt to catch the roadrunner.

Acme is a (barely) profitable small distributor, getting by on a bottom line just over 1% of sales—about ¼ of the average performance of a wholesale distributor. The company employs 28 sales reps—far more than a company this size ought to have—and this also (paradoxically) contributes to the company's profit challenges.

About WayPoint Analytics

I'll be using reports from WayPoint Analytics as a source of profit and performance information. If you don't use WayPoint, you can develop the source information using other methods and plug it into the workbook. I'll also be using the WayPoint ProfitComp™ sales pay system to illustrate how to load the results, and to produce sample pay statements and reports. I'm using WayPoint both because it's a convenient mechanism to show how this is done, and also because it's how I make a living, and I hope you'll consider adopting these systems for your own company. You can use this as a guide in duplicating the process for your own company, and your own pay system.

There is also a complete video set of the plan design process detailed in this section of the book. (See the appendix for the web location.)

Over the next few sections, I'll use the plan design workbook for Excel that's available for download as a companion to this book. (See the appendix for the web location.)

The objective of this section is to work through the real process of designing and implementing a functioning pay system.

Remember, the reason for creating a new plan is bring pay into line with results, and that means changing either the pay for given results, or the results for given pay.

As I work through the process, I'll be referring to the current pay results for the territories, but I'll keep this a secondary consideration. The primary purpose of the new plan is to deliver appropriately pay for the profit results being produced.

The general process will be:

1) get territory summary information into the workbook

2) rank the territories by pay as a percentage of NBC

3) identify a territory that best fits each of the first five scenarios (not all scenarios may be represented)

4) create a worksheet for each exemplar territory, and work out viable pay rates

5) use the NBC Pay Calculator to model the pay for the exemplar territories

6) group other territories that surround each identified scenario with the exemplar territory

7) where feasible, rebalance territories by moving accounts between territories to correct outliers

8) adjust pay parameters to get a "best fit"

Getting Started

Download and open the CompPlanDesign.xlsx workbook. (See the appendix for download location.) There are two workbooks in the set: one is already populated using the process described in this chapter; the other with no data, ready for you to use with your own information. You can follow along using the populated version.

Rep	Invoices	Revenue	GP		NBC		Net		Comp	Eff. Rate GP	NBC
Anders, Fred	1,076	$2,794,773	$479,344	17.2%	$272,540	9.8%	$151,265	5.4%	$121,275	25.30%	44.50%
Barnhill, Apryl	514	$1,167,169	$346,592	29.7%	$248,200	21.3%	$159,513	13.7%	$88,687	25.59%	35.73%
Bynum, Oretha	640	$363,643	$127,438	35.0%	($32,704)	(9.0%)	($71,502)	(19.7%)	$38,798	30.44%	118.63%
Campbell, Jocelyn	938	$2,313,082	$463,904	20.1%	$260,173	11.2%	$141,231	6.1%	$118,942	25.64%	45.72%
Coggins, James	2,338	$2,548,523	$668,620	26.2%	($95,641)	(3.8%)	($231,299)	(9.1%)	$135,658	20.29%	141.84%
Crider, Liana	484	$532,319	$148,042	27.8%	$57,688	10.8%	$12,705	2.4%	$44,983	30.39%	77.98%
Daley, Edyth	451	$847,095	$108,761	12.8%	$12,892	1.5%	($20,253)	(2.4%)	$33,145	30.48%	257.10%
Dennison, Luci	128	$268,704	$58,349	21.7%	$35,071	13.1%	$17,025	6.3%	$18,046	30.93%	51.45%
Dotson, Joel	117	$118,607	$35,857	30.2%	$7,391	6.2%	($3,420)	(2.9%)	$10,812	30.15%	146.28%
Frederick, Claudie	122	$123,447	$14,047	11.4%	($12,860)	(10.4%)	($17,348)	(14.1%)	$4,488	31.95%	34.90%
Fuller, Minh	468	$1,021,114	$262,066	25.7%	$199,008	19.5%	$132,516	13.0%	$66,492	25.37%	33.41%
Gomes, Nobuko	626	$1,061,134	$234,404	22.1%	$118,876	11.2%	$47,667	4.5%	$71,209	30.38%	59.90%
Guerrero, Robt	409	$221,015	$93,549	42.3%	($21,208)	(9.6%)	($49,497)	(22.4%)	$28,289	30.24%	133.39%
Hargrave, Karry	3	$1,186	$471	39.7%	($592)	(49.9%)	($735)	(62.0%)	$143	30.46%	24.24%
Kiser, Shiloh	69	$367,280	$56,286	15.3%	$36,796	10.0%	$19,900	5.4%	$16,895	30.02%	45.92%
Lake, Charles	247	$236,462	$66,330	28.1%	$27,302	11.5%	$7,146	3.0%	$20,156	30.39%	73.83%
McClure, Pamila	165	$292,864	$84,445	28.8%	$54,229	18.5%	$28,755	9.8%	$25,475	30.17%	46.98%
McMaster, Vonda	324	$410,729	$117,561	28.6%	$60,303	14.7%	$24,722	6.0%	$35,581	30.27%	59.00%
O'Connell, Marchelle	490	$549,991	$146,041	26.6%	$45,839	8.3%	$1,630	0.3%	$44,210	30.27%	96.44%
Orlando, Shalanda	63	$51,106	$15,102	29.6%	$4,431	8.7%	($198)	(0.4%)	$4,629	30.65%	104.47%
Pence, Branden	267	$339,948	$80,218	23.6%	$31,130	9.2%	$6,620	1.9%	$24,509	30.55%	78.73%
Posey, Joe	1,398	$905,329	$177,114	19.6%	($87,868)	(9.7%)	($141,660)	(15.6%)	$53,793	30.37%	61.22%
Royal, Noella	27	$35,045	$5,474	15.6%	$1,451	4.1%	($197)	(0.6%)	$1,648	30.11%	113.56%
Salerno, Britni	676	$1,627,940	$262,869	16.1%	$131,801	8.1%	$63,267	3.9%	$68,534	26.07%	52.00%
Schwarz, Jovita	1,141	$1,331,475	$275,318	20.7%	$80,165	6.0%	$9,999	0.8%	$70,167	25.49%	87.53%
Seeley, Damaris	112	$212,645	$44,140	20.8%	$23,040	10.8%	$9,592	4.5%	$13,447	30.46%	58.37%
Siegel, Alexia	50	$9,068	($1,562)	(17.2%)	($10,008)	(110.4%)	($10,008)	(110.4%)	$0	0.00%	0.00%
Townes, Olinda	446	$579,253	$116,241	20.1%	$38,607	6.7%	$2,663	0.5%	$35,944	30.92%	93.10%
	13,789	$20,330,947	$4,487,023	22.1%	$1,486,054	7.3%	$290,100	1.4%	$1,195,954	26.65%	80.48%

figure 7.01

The first thing that you want to pull from WayPoint is the Commission | Effective Rates report. This will inventory all of your sales territories, provide a sense of how those territories are performing, and show how they're being paid for that performance. Within the example, I'll select a full fiscal year because it will provides a broader picture of the business and most planning is done on an annual basis anyway.

After selecting a full year and going to the commission tab, you can pull the Effective Rates Report (figure 7.01) and have it exported into an Excel spreadsheet by pushing the Excel button at the top. This may prompt a warning that the report is in a web format rather than a standard Excel format.

ID	Rep	Invoices	Revenue	GP	%	NBC	%	Net	%	Comp	GP Rate	NBC Rate
420	Daley, Edyth	451	$847,095	$108,761	12.80%	$12,892	1.50%	($20,253)	-2.40%	$33,145	30.48%	257.10%
440	Dotson, Joel	117	$118,607	$35,857	30.20%	$7,391	6.20%	($3,420)	-2.90%	$10,812	30.15%	146.28%
430	Coggins, James	2,338	$2,548,523	$668,820	26.20%	($95,641)	-3.80%	($231,299)	-9.10%	$135,858	20.29%	141.84%
310	Guerrero, Robt	409	$221,015	$93,549	42.30%	($21,208)	-9.60%	($49,497)	-22.40%	$28,289	30.24%	133.39%
320	Bynum, Oretha	640	$363,643	$127,438	35.00%	($32,704)	-9.00%	($71,502)	-19.70%	$38,798	30.44%	118.63%
370	Royal, Noella	27	$35,045	$5,474	15.60%	$1,451	4.10%	($197)	-0.60%	$1,648	30.11%	113.56%
330	Orlando, Shalanda	63	$51,106	$15,102	29.60%	$4,431	8.70%	($198)	-0.40%	$4,629	30.65%	104.47%
380	O'Connell, Marchelle	490	$549,991	$146,041	26.60%	$45,839	8.30%	$1,630	0.30%	$44,210	30.27%	98.44%
OT	Townes, Olinda	446	$579,253	$116,241	20.10%	$38,607	6.70%	$2,663	0.50%	$35,944	30.92%	93.10%
500	Schwarz, Jovita	1,141	$1,331,475	$275,318	20.70%	$80,165	6.00%	$9,999	0.80%	$70,167	25.49%	87.53%
450	Pence, Branden	267	$339,948	$80,218	23.60%	$31,130	9.20%	$6,620	1.90%	$24,509	30.55%	78.73%
LC	Crider, Liana	484	$532,319	$148,042	27.80%	$57,688	10.80%	$12,705	2.40%	$44,983	30.39%	77.98%
340	Lake, Charles	247	$236,462	$66,330	28.10%	$27,302	11.50%	$7,146	3.00%	$20,156	30.39%	73.83%
100	Posey, Joe	1,398	$905,329	$177,114	19.60%	($87,868)	-9.70%	($141,660)	-15.60%	$53,793	30.37%	61.22%
510	Gomes, Nobuko	626	$1,061,134	$234,404	22.10%	$118,876	11.20%	$47,667	4.50%	$71,209	30.38%	59.90%
VM	McMaster, Vonda	324	$410,729	$117,561	28.60%	$60,303	14.70%	$24,722	6.00%	$35,581	30.27%	59.00%
480	Seeley, Damaris	112	$212,845	$44,140	20.80%	$23,040	10.80%	$9,592	4.50%	$13,447	30.46%	58.37%
390	Salerno, Britni	676	$1,627,940	$282,869	16.10%	$131,801	8.10%	$63,267	3.90%	$68,534	26.07%	52.00%
470	Dennison, Luci	128	$268,704	$58,349	21.70%	$35,071	13.10%	$17,025	6.30%	$18,046	30.93%	51.45%
460	McClure, Pamila	165	$292,864	$84,445	28.80%	$54,229	18.50%	$28,755	9.80%	$25,475	30.17%	46.98%
SK	Kiser, Shiloh	69	$367,280	$56,286	15.30%	$36,796	10.00%	$19,900	5.40%	$16,895	30.02%	45.92%
260	Campbell, Jocelyn	938	$2,313,082	$463,904	20.10%	$260,173	11.20%	$141,231	6.10%	$118,942	25.64%	45.72%
400	Anders, Fred	1,078	$2,794,773	$479,344	17.20%	$272,540	9.80%	$151,285	5.40%	$121,275	25.30%	44.50%
490	Barnhill, Apryl	514	$1,167,169	$346,592	29.70%	$248,200	21.30%	$159,513	13.70%	$88,687	25.59%	35.73%
410	Frederick, Claudie	122	$123,447	$14,047	11.40%	($12,860)	-10.40%	($17,348)	-14.10%	$4,488	31.95%	34.90%
MF	Fuller, Minh	468	$1,021,114	$262,066	25.70%	$199,008	19.50%	$132,516	13.00%	$66,492	25.37%	33.41%
550	Hargrave, Karry	3	$1,186	$471	39.70%	($592)	-49.90%	($735)	-62.00%	$143	30.46%	24.24%
300	Siegel, Alexia	50	$9,068	($1,562)	-17.20%	($10,008)	-110.40%	($10,008)	-110.40%	$0	0.00%	0.00%

EffRates / NBC Pay Calculator / Territory

figure 7.02

After hitting okay (provided you see the warning), you'll have a report that also has the sales territory numbers which you will need later on. Copy this sheet into the EffRates tab in the design workbook, then sort on the effective rates to make relative performance ranges easy to group. (I've removed the background fill and reset the borders to make it easier to read.) (figure 7.02)

Now is the time to look for six common scenarios that can occur in a company's performance. Not all companies will have all six, but each one is important and can have a significant impact on your business.

Scenario 1

The first case is where you have a balanced territory, where pay is in range of what you might expect or would like to have for the current profit performance.

This is the easiest scenario because all that you need to do is establish a new set of parameters to suit the new metrics which will deliver similar pay for similar performance. It's a pretty straightforward operation when you use the workbook.

Scenario 2

The second scenario involves a territory with a profit performance well above its current compensation; meaning that it's generating an NBC profit level well above what you'd expect for the current pay level of the territory. While you could easily just put that person on the new pay scheme, it could mean that their income would be doubled or tripled. This could be inappropriate for a number of reasons and I'll discuss how to treat this situation later on.

Scenario 3

The third scenario occurs when a territory's NBC isn't enough to account for what's being paid to the sales rep. The rep is either receiving the lion's share or, in extreme cases, all of the profits while the company is left with little (or nothing). Suffice it to say, in such a case there needs to be a more equitable split of the profits between the sales rep and the company. Part of the reason for adopting a new sales compensation plan is to avoid these situations and there will be some special mechanisms to transition these into the new plan.

Scenario 4

The fourth kind is so bad that the territory is actually losing money on operations alone. The territories have a negative NBC but the sales reps are still being paid. This is an extremely difficult situation that requires special measures which will usually take the form of territory realignments (swapping customers in and out of the territory) to ensure that there's enough potential profitability to give the sales rep a fighting chance to make things work.

Scenario 5

The fifth scenario involves a special territory which may only consist of a handful of accounts that are in some way unusual or different from most other customers. It may require a different kind of a pay scenario or even something that's completely outside of a normal profit-based plan. While you should always aim to adhere to a profit plan when possible, it's smart to have room for flexibility and creativity when it comes to mechanics.

Scenario 6

The sixth and final scenario is a highly specialized (and sometimes short-term) territory you might create where all of the accounts are large-scale money-losing accounts. This is most commonly used when a company is under-performing and, in this situation, a majority of the territories will be generating losses. It's not mathematically possible to put together a good profit-driven plan that pays sales reps when their territories are losing money.

The company needs to start generating a positive cash flow so it can get out of the hole and this will require some drastic changes. One of the techniques for resolving this kind of situation is to take a number of significant large-scale, money-losing accounts and put them in the hands of a specialist who will be paid on a completely different basis. (more on this later.)

Picking Representative Territories

Keeping those six scenarios in mind, you want to look at the plans and find the best way to segment them into those six categories.

You can do this by selecting the last line of the header of the table then do a quick sort on the last column (the NBC rate). In the example, sorting from largest to smallest NBC rate, I can see what percentage of the NBC is being paid to the sales rep. (figure 7.03)

Picking exemplars of the various performance levels of the territories gives a starting point for finding parameters that suit each one. These can then be used as a baseline model for territories at similar performance levels.

Let's take a look at an appropriately paid territory. As a general rule, most companies in wholesale distribution (whether they're on an NBC program or not) effectively pay something around 50% of the NBC to the sales force. If I look for a territory that's both within that range and has a reasonable scale (since territories with small revenues aren't representative of what I want), the most obvious one in the example is that of Britni Salerno seems like a good-sized territory paying near 50% of NBC. So I'll highlight the row for comparison purposes. I've also added a "1" for scenario 1 at the right end of the row. (figure 7.03)

Next I'll take a look for an underpaid territory. This is one where the territory is of a respectable size, but the rep is getting considerably less than the 50% range in terms of pay. April Barnhill is a good example because she manages a million dollar territory with $248,000 in NBC but she's only being paid 35% of it. This entry will be highlighted as well and marked as scenario 2.

	A	B	C	D	E	F	G	H	I	J	K	L	M	N
1	ID	Rep	Invoices	Revenue	GP	%	NBC	%	Net	%	Comp	GP Rate	NBC Rate	
2	420	Daley, Edyth	451	$847,095	$108,761	12.80%	$12,892	1.50%	($20,253)	-2.40%	$33,145	30.48%	257.1%	5
3	440	Dotson, Joel	117	$118,607	$35,857	30.20%	$7,391	6.20%	($3,420)	-2.90%	$10,812	30.15%	146.3%	
4	430	Coggins, James	2,338	$2,548,523	$668,620	26.20%	($95,641)	-3.80%	($231,299)	-9.10%	$135,658	20.29%	141.8%	4
5	310	Guerrero, Robt	409	$221,015	$93,549	42.30%	($21,208)	-9.60%	($49,497)	-22.40%	$28,289	30.24%	133.4%	
6	320	Bynum, Oretha	640	$363,643	$127,438	35.00%	($32,704)	-9.00%	($71,502)	-19.70%	$38,798	30.44%	118.6%	
7	370	Royal, Noella	27	$35,045	$5,474	15.60%	$1,451	4.10%	($197)	-0.60%	$1,648	30.11%	113.6%	
8	330	Orlando, Shalanda	63	$51,106	$15,102	29.60%	$4,431	8.70%	($198)	-0.40%	$4,629	30.65%	104.5%	
9	380	O'Connell, Marchelle	490	$549,991	$146,041	26.60%	$45,839	8.30%	$1,630	0.30%	$44,210	30.27%	96.4%	
10	OT	Townes, Olinda	446	$579,253	$116,241	20.10%	$38,607	6.70%	$2,663	0.50%	$35,944	30.92%	93.1%	
11	500	Schwarz, Jovita	1,141	$1,331,475	$275,318	20.70%	$80,165	6.00%	$9,999	0.80%	$70,167	25.49%	87.5%	3
12	450	Pence, Branden	267	$339,948	$80,218	23.60%	$31,130	9.20%	$6,620	1.90%	$24,509	30.55%	78.7%	
13	LC	Crider, Liana	484	$532,319	$148,042	27.80%	$57,688	10.80%	$12,705	2.40%	$44,983	30.39%	78.0%	
14	340	Lake, Charles	247	$236,462	$66,330	28.10%	$27,302	11.50%	$7,146	3.00%	$20,156	30.39%	73.8%	
15	100	Posey, Joe	1,398	$905,329	$177,114	19.60%	($87,868)	-9.70%	($141,660)	-15.60%	$53,793	30.37%	61.2%	
16	510	Gomes, Nobuko	626	$1,061,134	$234,404	22.10%	$118,876	11.20%	$47,667	4.50%	$71,209	30.38%	59.9%	
17	VM	McMaster, Vonda	324	$410,729	$117,561	28.60%	$60,303	14.70%	$24,722	6.00%	$35,581	30.27%	59.0%	
18	480	Seeley, Damaris	112	$212,645	$44,140	20.80%	$23,040	10.80%	$9,592	4.50%	$13,447	30.46%	58.4%	
19	470	Salerno, Britni	676	$1,627,940	$262,869	16.10%	$131,801	8.10%	$63,267	3.90%	$68,534	26.07%	52.0%	1
20	470	Dennison, Luci	128	$268,704	$58,349	21.70%	$35,071	13.10%	$17,025	6.30%	$18,046	30.93%	51.5%	
21	460	McClure, Pamila	165	$292,864	$84,445	28.80%	$54,229	18.50%	$28,755	9.80%	$25,475	30.17%	47.0%	
22	SK	Kiser, Shiloh	69	$367,280	$56,286	15.30%	$36,796	10.00%	$19,900	5.40%	$16,895	30.02%	45.9%	
23	260	Campbell, Jocelyn	938	$2,313,082	$463,904	20.10%	$260,173	11.20%	$141,231	6.10%	$118,942	25.64%	45.7%	
24	400	Anders, Fred	1,076	$2,794,773	$479,344	17.20%	$272,540	9.80%	$151,265	5.40%	$121,275	25.30%	44.5%	
25	490	Barnhill, Apryl	514	$1,167,169	$346,592	29.70%	$248,200	21.30%	$159,513	13.70%	$88,687	25.59%	35.7%	2
26	410	Frederick, Claudie	122	$123,447	$14,047	11.40%	($12,860)	-10.40%	($17,348)	-14.10%	$4,488	31.95%	34.9%	
27	MF	Fuller, Minh	468	$1,016,650	$329,068	32.37%	$266,855	26.25%	$132,516	13.03%	$66,492	20.21%	24.9%	

figure 7.03

The third territory that will be highlighted is one where the NBC is completely insufficient when compared to what the person is being paid. Jovita Schwarz is a good example because she's getting almost 90% of the NBC, and so it's highlighted and marked with scenario 3.

The next example will be one where there's a completely negative NBC yet I'm paying a rep. James Coggins is probably the best example because his territory is generating around $2.5 million in revenue yet the company is taking a $95,000 NBC loss. This is marked as scenario 4.

As far as a specialist territory is concerned, I know from previous research that Edyth Daley is a good example. She has a territory consisting of only two accounts, and these are quite different from the company's typical customer. I'll mark the row as scenario 5.

This particular spreadsheet doesn't include an example of a scenario 6 – one composed entirely of money-losers that a specialist is trying to reform. This is almost always a specially-created territory that's a result of this process.

I now have exemplars for first 5 kinds of territories. These exemplars will be examined one by one to show you how to come up with the right metrics or parameters for each scenario. I'll begin this process by preparing a territory tab for each of the five examples that were flagged earlier. These examples are going to help develop appropriate models for a pay system.

Examining the Territories

I need to create a tab for each of the exemplar territories I've selected. Do this is to right-click the "Territory" tab, select "Move or Copy," and then highlight the option to have it moved to the end. (figure 7.04) It's worth saving an extra blank sheet just in case you want to work in it later. I'm going to name each sheet (or tab) for the salesperson that the model will be based on.

Let's start by pulling the report for Salerno. I'll go into WayPoint and select Salerno's name then run her Customer | NBC Ranking Report. (figure 7.05) I export the report into

Excel, copy its contents, then right-click, select the Paste Special option and then check "Values" so it doesn't change the format for any of the fields.

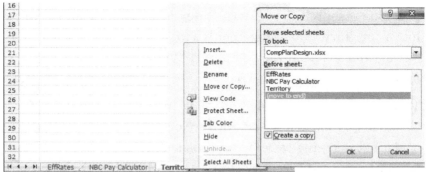

figure 7.04

Working from the initial numbers on the EffRates tab, I put an approximation of Salerno's total pay ($68,500) into the yellow Target Pay box and set the base pay portion to $12,000 ($1,000 per month). (figure 7.06)

		Revenue		GP		GM%	NBC		Net	Invoices		Qty	
	Customer	$	/ inv	$	/ inv		$	accum		Total	-NBC	Qty	NBC/
1	I Party Retail Store	1,040,103	3,810	122,682	449	11.8%	76,402	76,402	40,868	273	19%	11,885,237	0.01
2	Premier Seating Company	207,863	1,777	59,261	507	28.5%	32,345	108,747	18,855	117	43%	7,486,464	0.00
3	Westover Companies	246,702	1,240	49,865	251	20.2%	10,010	118,757	(3,763)	199	56%	120,746	0.08
4	Prestige Delivery Systems Inc	50,354	2,650	10,463	551	20.8%	7,606	126,363	5,281	19	32%	47,296	0.16
5	Beverage Equipment Supply Inc	24,767	2,477	6,112	611	24.7%	3,686	130,049	3,686	10	0%	53,543	0.07
6	Farmers & Traders Lf Insur Co	18,627	1,433	4,691	361	25.2%	3,003	133,052	1,865	13	38%	336,007	0.01
7	Inter-City Fish Co Inc	14,069	14,069	2,775	2,775	19.7%	2,455	135,507	1,802	1	0%	2	10.00
8	Capital Bluecross	4,333	4,333	1,420	1,420	32.8%	1,246	136,753	912	1	0%	7	10.00
9	Converium Centre Inc	1,514	1,514	469	469	30.9%	337	137,089	232	1	0%	2	10.00
10	Royal Harvest Foods	1,728	1,728	436	436	25.2%	319	137,408	222	1	0%	600	0.53
11	Windsor Manufacturing Co Inc	2,879	2,879	565	565	19.6%	302	137,710	176	1	0%	36	8.38
12	Thomas Black Corporation	1,515	505	442	147	29.2%	91	137,801	(34)	3	0%	12	7.54
13	Transamerica Holdings LLC	92	92	18	18	20.0%	(185)	137,616	(189)	1	100%	1	(10.00)
14	Choate Hall & Stewart	0	0	0	0	.0%	(202)	137,414	(202)	1	100%	(1)	10.00
15	Bio-Rad Micromeasurements	2,041	408	456	91	22.3%	(216)	137,198	(320)	5	100%	901	(0.24)
16	Good Cause Marketing Inc	(75)	(75)	(34)	(34)	44.9%	(235)	136,963	(227)	1	100%	(2)	10.00
17	The Rouse Company	(112)	(112)	(112)	(112)	100.0%	(463)	136,500	(438)	1	100%	(101)	4.59
18	Federal Metal Co Inc	5,631	563	1,506	151	26.7%	(656)	135,844	(993)	10	90%	1,137	(0.58)
19	Global Business Consulting, Inc	1,883	314	448	75	23.8%	(1,466)	134,378	(1,576)	6	100%	1,081	(1.36)
20	G-S Company Inc	4,027	336	1,408	117	35.0%	(2,577)	131,801	(2,892)	12	100%	665	(3.88)

figure 7.05

The worksheet uses these numbers to start modeling the territory. Repeat these steps for the other exemplar territories, adding target pay and base pay amounts for each.

Now I have spreadsheets set up for each of the territories: there's the Salerno spreadsheet (for the appropriately paid territory); Barnhill (underpaid); Schwarz (overpaid); Coggins (negative NBC); and Daley (specialized territory).

	A	B	C	D	E	F	G	H	P	Q	R	T
1										Target Pay		$68,500
2										Annual Base		$12,000
3										Territory NBC		$131,802
4												
5		Customer	Rev $	/ inv	GP $	/ inv	GM%	NBC $		accum NBC		NBC Rate
6	367	I Party Retail Store	1,040,103	3,810	122,682	449	11.8%	76,402		76,402	✔	74.0%
7	1157	Premier Seating Company	207,863	1,777	59,261	507	28.5%	32,345		108,747	✔	52.0%
8	6395	Westover Companies	246,702	1,240	49,865	251	20.2%	10,010		118,757	✔	47.6%
9	1072	Prestige Delivery Systems Inc	50,354	2,650	10,463	551	20.8%	7,606		126,363	✔	44.7%
10	966	Beverage Equipment Supply Inc	24,767	2,477	6,112	611	24.7%	3,686		130,049	✔	43.4%
11	1225	Farmers & Traders Lf Insur Co	18,627	1,433	4,691	361	25.2%	3,003		133,052	✔	42.5%
12	1573	Inter-City Fish Co Inc	14,069	14,069	2,775	2,775	19.7%	2,455		135,507	✔	41.7%
13	1574	Capital Bluecross	4,333	4,333	1,420	1,420	32.8%	1,246		136,753	✔	41.3%
14	1513	Converium Centre Inc	1,514	1,514	469	469	30.9%	337		137,090	✔	41.2%
15	1343	Royal Harvest Foods	1,728	1,728	436	436	25.2%	319		137,409	✔	41.1%
16	1506	Windsor Manufacturing Co Inc	2,879	2,879	565	565	19.6%	302		137,711	✔	41.0%
17	1127	Thomas Black Corporation	1,515	505	442	147	29.2%	91		137,802	✔	41.0%
18	9999	Transamerica Holdings LLC	92	92	18	18	20.0%	(185)		137,617	✔	41.1%
19	4981	Choate Hall & Stewart	0	0	0	0	0.0%	(202)		137,415	✔	41.1%
20	1016	Bio-Rad Micromeasurements	2,041	408	456	91	22.3%	(216)		137,199	✔	41.2%
21	627	Good Cause Marketing Inc	(75)	(75)	(34)	(34)	44.9%	(235)		136,964	✔	41.3%
22	5617	The Rouse Company	(112)	(112)	(112)	(112)	100.0%	(463)		136,501	✔	41.4%
23	1373	Federal Metal Co Inc	5,631	563	1,506	151	26.7%	(656)		135,845	✔	41.6%
24	1687	Global Business Consulting, Inc	1,883	314	448	75	23.8%	(1,466)		134,379	✔	42.0%
25	6564	G-S Company Inc	4,027	336	1,408	117	35.0%	(2,577)		131,802	✔	42.9%
26										131,802	✔	42.9%
27										131,802	✔	43.0%

figure 7.06

Finally I'll create a tab, and name it "Turnaround" territory.

With all of these territories laid out like this, it should also be easy to do some territory realignments as I go along. The turnaround tab will be used when I need to move accounts out of territories in order to bring them into a mathematically-workable condition. The turnaround tab can be used as a temporary or perhaps permanent destination of the accounts I remove.

The next step involves using the NBC calculator. This is a place where I can do some rough estimates of what the numbers ought to be for each one of these sales reps. Let's start our testing with Salerno because her territory is pretty much in line with what I want.

I start by going to into the effective rates sheet and copy the values from her row. I right-click and "Paste Special" (selecting "Values" and checking "Transpose") so only the values are inserted and I want to take values from a row and paste them into a column. (figure 7.07)

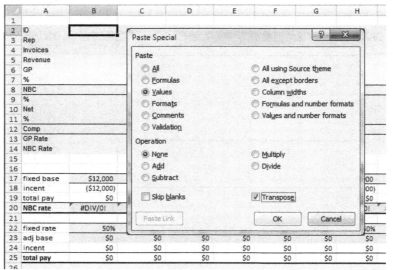

figure 7.07

That information will be pasted into field to the right of "ID" as shown and all of the values will show down the column.

I then repeat this process for each of the remaining four scenarios (in the previously established order). When this is finished, I have the five sales reps' information lined up at the top of the screen. Down below are three blocks which give us some idea of what the numbers will mean and allow us to do some "what ifs?" with the numbers.

The green rows at the end of each block are the output; the results of your "what if?" scenarios. The yellow rows are where you input or modify the numbers in the system in order to give you those results.

In the first block, I can set any kind of a fixed base pay in the yellow cell, and it will calculate how much incentive is needed to match the original pay as well as the required NBC commission rate to get that incentive amount.

The second block is where I can enter an NBC commission rate, and this block will then tell us what the base needs to be in order to achieve the previous compensation. Sometimes the numbers you plug in will turn out nonsensical results which will tell you that the number you used isn't possible or viable.

	A	B
1		
2	ID	390
3	Rep	Salerno
4	Invoices	676
5	Revenue	$1,627,940
6	GP	$262,869
7	%	16.10%
8	NBC	$131,801
9	%	8.10%
10	Net	$63,267
11	%	3.90%
12	Comp	$68,534
13	GP Rate	26.07%
14	NBC Rate	52.00%
15		
16		
17	fixed base	$12,000
18	incent	$56,534
19	total pay	$68,534
20	NBC rate	42.9%
21		
22	fixed rate	50%
23	adj base	$2,634
24	incent	$65,901
25	total pay	$68,534
26		
27	NBC rate	40%
28	comm	$52,720
29	base	$12,000
30	total pay	$64,720
31	variance	-3,814
32	NBC%	49.1%
33		

figure 7.08

Finally, the third block allows you to plug in both the NBC rate and the base rate. The results then show what the total pay would have been, were the entered parameters in use during that year.

It also shows the variance between what was paid and what would have been paid if the company was using the plan. It also shows what percentage of the NBC goes to the sales rep.

Using industry-wide pay practices, this would be roughly 50%. Your particular targets may vary—use your best judgment.

Our objective is something in the neighborhood of 50% for the rep, which leaves the other 50% for the company. Sharing equally just seems like basic fairness, and top profit-producing companies usually have plans that pay something under 50%.

Pay plans that give significantly more to the sales force than to the company are a sign of an over-sized sales force and a dysfunctional sales model. (This is not uncommon—on average, most distribution companies have a sales force evolved from a time of high-growth, and are too large for a low-growth mature market.)

Scenario 1 Model

Once again, let's start with Salerno where I already have a territory which is both performing well and paying appropriately. If I had no base pay, the NBC rate would be about 52%. I can set that at 50% to reflect a good target plan rate.

However, I'd like to have a base pay in my proposed pay plan.

There are a number of mechanical reasons and some science for this idea. First, a base reduces the amount of variability in the compensation from period to period. This is especially valuable for companies where the business is highly seasonable. For instance, a company that sells golfing supplies may do well in summer but there won't be much business during winter when sales may drop off almost entirely. If reps aren't making any money during the winter months, then they're far more likely to quit. By increasing the amount of base pay, reps will be paid enough that they'll be okay even in a slow season, and the lower commission rate will fund the base through lower total pay in the high season.

I probably want to do that anywhere there's a lot of fluctuation in sales—where the numbers can be really up or down throughout the year. Having a higher proportion of the pay coming from the base will help to smooth that out.

With this example, the company isn't seasonal so I can get away with a lower base. I'm contemplating having something along the lines of $1,000 or $2,000 per month as a base salary. If I plug in $24,000 as a base, I won't be paying such a large commission rate on the NBC so I don't overpay. Instead, I'm looking for a rate that (combined with the base salary) is going to deliver something close to 50% of the total NBC, so I'm going to test out a 30% NBC rate. The territory then comes down by around $5,000 and the rep's overall share works out to 48%.

If I want to get that number closer to 50%, I can either increase the base pay or the NBC rate. In this case, I chose to raise the NBC to 32.5% which changes the rep's overall share to 50.7%. This is just a little under what the rep was earning and it's probably acceptable. However, I'll increase that number to 35%; the result is a little more than the rep was paid before, but this territory is being well-managed and is a model for how I want other territories to operate. I feel that giving a slight increase to somebody in a well-performing territory will be a good way to get other salespeople enthusiastic about the new program. As such, I'm perfectly willing to invest an extra $1,600 for the same performance in that territory.

Scenario 2 Model

Barnhill, the rep for the next territory, is being underpaid. The company is only paying out 35% of the total NBC instead of the expected 50%. This is a high-performing territory where the rep should be rightfully rewarded; if all of the company's territories looked like this, its financial statements would be greatly improved. As with Salerno, it's probably a good idea to pay Barnhill more.

I'll just leave the $24,000 base pay in place. I'm not sure if it's going to be a policy yet, but it's a good starting point. I begin by testing out the same 35% NBC rate that I used for Salerno. Looking at the results, this high-performing territory is going to pay the rep $22,000 more than her previous rate. It's using the same parameters as a good operating territory and it's certainly a great model for other territories, but I'm not sure that I want to have that much of a bump in pay. I may decide to selectively take territories like this one and either pay a lower base or a lower NBC rate so that the company can retain more of the available profits. I may also tie an eventually increase in this rate to bring it back to other territories getting into line so I have money to fund them. It wouldn't be good for the company's profitability if I gave huge increases to some of the territories and left the under-performers at a rate similar to what they're being paid now. If I contemplate having a transitional plan then I'll likely have to account for these territories in the plan.

Scenario 3 Model

In this third scenario (Schwarz), where the vast majority of a territory's NBC is being given to the rep with little actually going to the company, the territory itself isn't good at the moment. In trying to figure out what rates might be appropriate for this territory, I need to be both brutally honest and brutally efficient. I can try reducing the fixed rate to 20% of NBC and see what that does to the base, but that exercise is better suited to when I already have an acceptable NBC. Instead, I want pay that's in line with what the NBC *should* be.

Under the scenario that I'm looking at, the rep would be paid, say, 70% of the NBC instead of the 87.5% she's being paid now. However, I'm going to change the NBC rate to 35% and leave the $24,000 base. The territory would now be paying out $52,000 instead of $70,000. That's still roughly 65% of the total NBC so the rate would need to be reduced even further. I would need to lower the base pay a bit if I wanted to max this at 60% of the NBC. By reducing the base pay to $20,000, the rep would now make 59.9% of the NBC.

Bear in mind that this is still a working number and I'm not finished getting to the appropriate pay level for the territory. I'll return to this in the next phase, and use territory balancing to bring the this territory into a workable condition.

Scenario 4 Model

In Coggins' case, the entire territory is underwater. The company has lost $231,000 in the territory before even paying the sales rep and then, compounding those losses, Coggins was paid $135,000. This is an all too common scenario where companies have been paying using old school methods of gross profit dollars and haven't been managing the cost to serve at all. Almost any company with this happening is going to have a number of territories that look like Coggins' does, and they absolutely destroy the company's ability to make money until they're corrected.

So how do I correct this? Let's do a little more modeling here. As was the case with Schwarz, I'm not trying to maintain the old pay rates so the first two blocks aren't useful at the moment. Instead, I'll focus on the third block. Even if you zeroed out the base pay, there's still no way to make this territory profitable. (You can't multiply a negative NBC by any rate and get a positive pay.) This is a scenario that needs to be solved on a different sheet which I'll discuss in the next section.

Scenario 5 Model

Next up is Daley who is being paid to do some very specialized business. Unfortunately, this territory is also underwater which means I have to work it on it on another sheet, like the previous scenarios.

Balancing Territories

Having outlined the basics, it's time to do some detailed work on each territory to bring things into line. I have the information and details as to what was sold to each customer and for how much in these tabs.

At the top-right of the screen, I can input a target pay and an annual base amount. The system will then provide some interesting information about what's going on in the territory which should provide some guidance on what to do next.

Scenario 1 Territory

Taking the numbers for the Scenario 1 territory (Salerno) from the NBC Pay Calculator tab, I can see that she had a total pay package near $68,500, and I'm looking for a $24,000 fixed base and a 35% NBC rate. For modeling purposes, the target pay I'll enter on the Salerno Territory sheet is $70,000 and the base is $24,000. The sheet then shows that the total territory NBC is $131,802, the commission rate is 35%, and she's getting 53% of the territory's total NBC. (figure 7.09)

The customer column shows all of the accounts that Salerno sold to during the year. There are a couple of other factors here like gross profit and gross margin, but the most important one is NBC. The block on the right-hand side gives us the ability to do some modeling; however, the number that I should focus on is the accumulated NBC. This column adds up the total volume going down row by row until I see at the bottom that the total accumulated NBC is the previously mentioned $131,802. The appropriate NBC rate to the right of this column changes as well, letting us know that the rate required to meet her target pay is 34.9% which is extremely close to the 35% that was selected earlier.

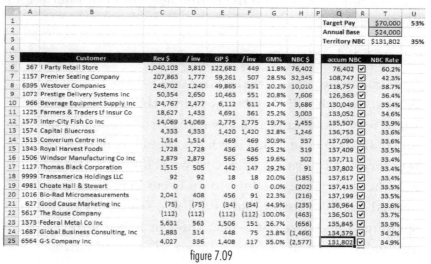

	A	B	C	D	E	F	G	H	P	Q	R	T	U
1										Target Pay		$70,000	53%
2										Annual Base		$24,000	
3										Territory NBC		$131,802	35%
4													
5		Customer	Rev $	/ inv	GP $	/ inv	GM%	NBC $		accum NBC		NBC Rate	
6	367	I Party Retail Store	1,040,103	3,810	122,682	449	11.8%	76,402		76,402	☑	60.2%	
7	1157	Premier Seating Company	207,863	1,777	59,261	507	28.5%	32,345		108,747	☑	42.3%	
8	6395	Westover Companies	246,702	1,240	49,865	251	20.2%	10,010		118,757	☑	38.7%	
9	1072	Prestige Delivery Systems Inc	50,354	2,650	10,463	551	20.8%	7,606		126,363	☑	36.4%	
10	966	Beverage Equipment Supply Inc	24,767	2,477	6,112	611	24.7%	3,686		130,049	☑	35.4%	
11	1225	Farmers & Traders Lf Insur Co	18,627	1,433	4,691	361	25.2%	3,003		133,052	☑	34.6%	
12	1573	Inter-City Fish Co Inc	14,069	14,069	2,775	2,775	19.7%	2,455		135,507	☑	33.9%	
13	1574	Capital Bluecross	4,333	4,333	1,420	1,420	32.8%	1,246		136,753	☑	33.6%	
14	1513	Converium Centre Inc	1,514	1,514	469	469	30.9%	337		137,090	☑	33.6%	
15	1343	Royal Harvest Foods	1,728	1,728	436	436	25.2%	319		137,409	☑	33.5%	
16	1506	Windsor Manufacturing Co Inc	2,879	2,879	565	565	19.6%	302		137,711	☑	33.4%	
17	1127	Thomas Black Corporation	1,515	505	442	147	29.2%	91		137,802	☑	33.4%	
18	9999	Transamerica Holdings LLC	92	92	18	18	20.0%	(185)		137,617	☑	33.4%	
19	4981	Choate Hall & Stewart	0	0	0	0	0.0%	(202)		137,415	☑	33.5%	
20	1016	Bio-Rad Micromeasurements	2,041	408	456	91	22.3%	(216)		137,199	☑	33.5%	
21	627	Good Cause Marketing Inc	(75)	(75)	(34)	(34)	44.9%	(235)		136,964	☑	33.6%	
22	5617	The Rouse Company	(112)	(112)	(112)	(112)	100.0%	(463)		136,501	☑	33.7%	
23	1373	Federal Metal Co Inc	5,631	563	1,506	151	26.7%	(656)		135,845	☑	33.9%	
24	1687	Global Business Consulting, Inc	1,883	314	448	75	23.8%	(1,466)		134,379	☑	34.2%	
25	6564	G-S Company Inc	4,027	336	1,408	117	35.0%	(2,577)		131,802	☑	34.9%	

figure 7.09

This shows us that I've found the factors that produce appropriate pay for this performance level.

Scenario 2 Territory

Next, I'll take a look at Barnhill, who is earning a lot less than she should for her profit performance my new profit-based program. Taking the total pay and commission rate numbers from the NBC Pay Calculator sheet, I have a target pay of $70,000 and a base pay of $24,000 which will be plugged into the territory sheet. The territory generates $248,199 and pay is 28% of territory NBC at a 18.5%

commission rate. This is pretty far from the 35% "standard" rate I worked out for Scenario 1..

Most likely, I'll bring this territory into line by giving Barnhill some more challenging (money-losing) accounts to work on. This can help the territory to be a better fit for the "normal" rates developed for Scenario 1. I'll move on to the next scenarios, where I'll likely find accounts I can move into this territory.

Scenario 3 Territory

Let's go back to the pay calculator and get the numbers for Schwarz which will then be input into the modeling sheet. Right now I'm looking at a pay package of around $48,000 and a $20,000 base. This is what I should be paying for the territory but I have a person who was making $70,000. It wouldn't be practical to immediately cut Schwarz's pay by around $22,000, but I could establish a transitory period spanning the course of the next three or four quarters to gradually ease into the new number. This would give Schwarz an opportunity to work within her territory to bring the expenses into line which would improve the territory's NBC and, in turn, help to maintain her pay rates.

I can also work the problem through territory realignment.

Transferring Schwarz's pay numbers of $70,000 target pay, $20,000 base and 35% commission, I can begin working on the account list.

Schwarz has a fairly large territory, one that's probably too large for a direct rep. There are also a few things going on in this territory. One of the accounts, American Automar Inc, is a very large gross profit producer that loses the company

$13,000. It's a customer that I might consider moving into another territory to make Schwarz's territory more viable.

I can model this by clearing the checkbox on the row for American Automar account. This causes the model to ignore this account for the purposes of the model.

I'll do the same for every account with GP less than $1,000. (In my opinion, accounts at this level should be served using a service model specific to small-volume accounts—a model that doesn't include sales coverage of commissions reps.)

I'll move American Automar to Barnhill's territory by copying the left block from the row to Barnhill's sheet, and then deleting it here.

This doesn't do enough to bring the territory into line, so I'll come back later.

Scenario 4 Territory

Next on the agenda is Coggins' territory. This territory is problematic because it's an example of the most difficult thing that I'm going to have to work around which is a territory that's flat-out losing money.

Let's start by looking at Coggins' current numbers on the NBC Calculator sheet. The pay package he has is around $135,000 and the base pay that I've been using is $24,000. When that information is inserted, I learn that the territory is $95,000 underwater. There are a number of things I need to do and that starts by seeing what's in the territory by switching to Coggins' territory sheet.

One of the things that I should avoid is assigning reps to the very small accounts which can never make money. Reps shouldn't call on these accounts because it's a waste of time.

With a money-losing territory, the first step might be taking out all the accounts producing under, say, $1,000 of GP per year. Anything under $1,000 probably isn't appropriate for a sales rep to be managing so I put the cursor on the header row of the list, sort by GP$ (large to small) and clear the customers with under $1,000 of GP. To get back the original order I re-sort by NBC$.

The NBC of this territory peaks at just over $92,000, generating about of $46,000 of earnings for the rep responsible for it—far below the $135,000 the company is paying.

To get an idea of what the NBC potential might be, I can divide the total NBC from the positive-NBC accounts into the revenue of the same group, giving a 5.1% rate of NBC production from revenue. If I apply this rate to the revenue total of the negative-NBC accounts, I can see that the territory could produce another $55,000 of NBC if the money losing accounts could be converted to money-making.

If this is done, I could add the $55,000 to the $92,000 from the profit-positive accounts, and have a territory producing NBC of $147,000 and paying $135,000 of it to the rep. (!!!)

This is not the fault of the rep.

Up until now, the company has been unaware of the real profit and pay dynamics of the territory, and has been effectively paying the rep to lose money.

The solution here isn't likely to be purely mechanical or mathematical. There are a number of approaches that can be considered and combined to correct the territory issue:

- ✓ develop a plan for the rep to address the loss-driving factors for each of the significant accounts

©2015 Randy MacLean

- ✓ dismantle the territory and reassign the high-GP accounts
- ✓ balance the territory by moving accounts to and from other territories
- ✓ use the territory as a base for a new Turnaround territory, where many or most significant money-losing accounts are put in the hands of a specialist who is paid on loss-reduction

Using some of these ideas, I can look at some of the significant money-losers at the bottom of the sheet which I may take out of the territory. Doing so on the worksheet, the territory still has a negative $56,000 NBC. It will be difficult to fix that without taking all of the money-losers out of the territory. I want to leave Coggins with some accounts to turn around himself which is why I'm only going to remove the accounts that lose more than $5,000 (taking them out then pasting special into the turnaround sheet). This doesn't solve the problem so I would need to add profitable accounts to the territory. Even if you took all of the money-losers out of the territory, however, there's only $92,000 in NBC so I'd have to give Coggins more than the entire NBC from the territory to maintain his pay level. As such, this presents a substantial challenge.

I may need to solve this by using some other territories that haven't been loaded into the system yet. I may even consider making a tab for each major territory so that I can reassign some accounts. However, this is as far as I can go with Coggins at the moment. There's a lot of money in the territory and, should the accounts be brought in line, those customers may eventually contribute a large amount of NBC.

Scenario 5 Territory

Finally, it's time to take a look at Daly's territory. Daly is a highly specialized rep who handles a certain kind of business. This rep has one really major account which isn't generating much money. What I may do is just leave this territory alone or find another way to take a look at the profitability. However, there may not be a good direct mechanic for this territory based on its nature.

Scenario 6 Territory

This type of territory may need to be created when a company has just too many money-losing accounts to allow for all of them to be included in profit-producing territories.

It's also a good strategy for a company that wants to focus on a fast profit turn-around.

	ID	Rep	Invoices	Revenue	GP	%	NBC	%	Net	%	Comp	GP Rate	NBC Rate	N
2	420	Daley, Edyth	451	$847,095	$108,761	12.80%	$12,892	1.50%	($20,253)	-2.40%	$33,145	30.48%	257.1%	5
3	440	Dotson, Joel	117	$118,607	$35,857	30.20%	$7,391	6.20%	($3,420)	-2.90%	$10,812	30.15%	146.3%	4
4	430	Coggins, James	2,338	$2,548,523	$668,620	26.20%	($95,641)	-3.80%	($231,299)	-9.10%	$135,658	20.29%	141.8%	4
5	310	Guerrero, Robt	409	$221,015	$93,549	42.30%	($21,208)	-9.60%	($49,497)	-22.40%	$28,289	30.24%	133.4%	4
6	320	Bynum, Oretha	640	$363,643	$127,438	35.00%	($32,704)	-9.00%	($71,502)	-19.70%	$38,798	30.44%	118.6%	4
7	370	Royal, Noella	27	$35,045	$5,474	15.60%	$1,451	4.10%	($197)	-0.60%	$1,648	30.11%	113.6%	4
8	330	Orlando, Shalanda	63	$51,106	$15,102	29.60%	$4,431	8.70%	($198)	-0.40%	$4,629	30.65%	104.5%	4
9	380	O'Connell, Marchelle	490	$549,991	$146,041	26.60%	$45,839	8.30%	$1,630	0.30%	$44,210	30.27%	96.4%	3
10	OT	Townes, Olinda	446	$579,253	$116,241	20.10%	$38,607	6.70%	$2,863	0.50%	$35,944	30.92%	93.1%	3
11	500	Schwarz, Jovita	1,141	$1,331,475	$275,318	20.70%	$80,165	6.00%	$9,999	0.80%	$70,167	25.49%	87.5%	3
12	450	Pence, Branden	267	$339,948	$80,218	23.60%	$31,130	9.20%	$6,620	1.90%	$24,509	30.55%	78.7%	3
13	LC	Crider, Liana	484	$532,319	$148,042	27.80%	$57,688	10.80%	$12,705	2.40%	$44,983	30.39%	78.0%	3
14	340	Lake, Charles	247	$236,462	$66,330	28.10%	$27,302	11.50%	$7,146	3.00%	$20,156	30.39%	73.8%	3
15	100	Posey, Joe	1,398	$905,329	$177,114	19.60%	($87,868)	-9.70%	($141,660)	-15.60%	$53,793	30.37%	61.2%	4
16	510	Gomes, Nobuko	626	$1,061,134	$234,404	22.10%	$118,876	11.20%	$47,667	4.50%	$71,209	30.38%	59.9%	1
17	VM	McMaster, Vonda	324	$410,729	$117,561	28.60%	$60,303	14.70%	$24,722	6.00%	$35,581	30.27%	59.0%	1
18	480	Seeley, Damaris	112	$212,645	$44,140	20.80%	$23,040	10.80%	$9,592	4.50%	$13,447	30.46%	58.4%	1
19	390	Salerno, Britni	676	$1,627,940	$262,869	16.10%	$131,801	8.10%	$63,267	3.90%	$68,534	26.07%	52.0%	1
20	470	Dennison, Luci	128	$268,704	$58,349	21.70%	$35,071	13.10%	$17,025	6.30%	$18,046	30.93%	51.5%	1
21	460	McClure, Pamla	165	$292,864	$84,445	28.80%	$54,229	18.50%	$28,755	9.80%	$25,475	30.17%	47.0%	1
22	SK	Kiser, Shiloh	69	$367,280	$56,286	15.30%	$36,796	10.00%	$19,900	5.40%	$16,895	30.02%	45.9%	1
23	260	Campbell, Jocelyn	938	$2,313,082	$463,904	20.10%	$260,173	11.20%	$141,231	6.10%	$118,942	25.64%	45.7%	1
24	400	Anders, Fred	1,076	$2,794,773	$479,344	17.20%	$272,540	9.80%	$151,265	5.40%	$121,275	25.30%	44.5%	1
25	490	Barnhill, Apryl	514	$1,167,169	$346,592	29.70%	$248,200	21.30%	$159,513	13.70%	$88,687	25.59%	35.7%	2
26	410	Frederick, Claudie	122	$123,447	$14,047	11.40%	($12,860)	-10.40%	($17,348)	-14.10%	$4,488	31.95%	34.9%	2
27	MF	Fuller, Minh	468	$1,016,650	$329,068	32.37%	$266,855	26.25%	$132,516	13.03%	$86,492	24.9%	24.9%	2
28	550	Hargrave, Karry	3	$1,186	$471	39.70%	($592)	49.90%	($735)	62.00%	$143	30.46%	24.2%	

figure 7.10

Territory Groups

Once I've built the most functional models I can for each of the example territories, my next task is to pull the territories similar to each of them into groups.

Going by the NBC Rate column, I include the territories similar to types 1, 2 & 3 into each of those groups. For type 4, I do the same and also include territory 100 because, like the others, it has negative NBC. (figure 7.10)

In a business where sales pay is near a nominal 50% of NBC, all that would be left is to continue the territory rebalancing process and fine-tune the rates.

In this business, the sales force has been funded at a level beyond its profit production, and is larger and/or over-paid.

Fixing this will require another significant step…

Rationalizing the Sales Force

Sales force rationalization is a necessary and recurring process in the evolution of every business. If a company annually reviews what it pays for profit production, and makes small course corrections, it occurs at an evolutionary rate.

If left unmanaged for too long, the market will eventually force the company to make revolutionary changes that will require much more courage.

The rationalization process will:
1) determine the budget available for sales pay
2) determine the number of, and pay levels for territories

3) choose the rep for each territory
4) assign accounts to each territory

Sales Force Reductions

If the company's sales pay was operating in the "normal" range: rep pay would total somewhere around 50% of NBC; sales reps would be paid at or slightly above industry-average for their performance; and the very few exceptions would be in territories where the company was establishing new or strategic business.

If the company has this kind of situation, the work of creating a good plan that will work for the company and the reps is practically done.

In this case, however, it's mathematically impossible to distribute the accounts in any way that produces viable pay for this many reps—and shares the NBC with the company on a more equitable basis.

In preparing for this walk-through process, I intentionally created a situation where the company is viable, but is seriously over-paying for sales coverage. Any small change in the market will instantly plunge this company into losses— likely a substantial risk today, as past market ripples have caused it to dip deep into its operating line or other financing resources, and that severely limit options to support losses. For its survival, it would be forced to rationalize the sales force.

I did this to ensure I'd be working in the most challenging environment for creating a new plan to help the company to greater profitability.

The company has more sales reps than it needs, or can afford, and territory alignments must include another step—sales force reduction.

Determine the Sales Comp Budget

To get a dispassionate overview, I created an extra spreadsheet. Pulling the totals from effective rates worksheet, I can see the company is paying 77% of the NBC to the sales reps. I added a couple of budget columns and worked out how much total pay would be available at a more normal 50%, and also at a transitional 60%. (figure 7.11)

	A	B	C	D	E	F
1						
2		current	budget	budget		
3	Revenue	$20,326,482	$20,326,482	$20,326,482		
4	GP	$4,554,023	$4,554,023	$4,554,023		
5	NBC	$1,553,899	$1,553,899	$1,553,899		
6	Net	$290,099	$776,950	$621,560		
7						
8	Comp	$1,195,955	$776,950	$932,339		
9	Comp % NBC	77.0%	50.0%	60.0%		
10						
11	Rep 1		$125,000	$125,000		
12	Rep 2		$110,000	$110,000		
13	Rep 3		$110,000	$110,000		
14	Rep 4		$85,000	$85,000		
15	Rep 5		$75,000	$85,000		
16	Rep 6		$75,000	$75,000		
17	Rep 7		$65,000	$75,000		
18	Rep 8		$65,000	$75,000		
19	Rep 9		$65,000	$65,000		
20	Rep 10			$65,000		
21	Rep 11			$65,000		
22			$775,000	$935,000		
23						

figure 7.11

Rep Count and Pay Levels

To evaluate what a right-sized force might look like at both these levels, I added some generic reps at pay levels similar to what the company is paying top reps currently.

This gives me a sense of how many reps "right-sized" sales force can fund with sales compensation budgets closer to industry norms.

Choosing the Reps

A useful exercise to guide in selecting how reps will be deployed is to place each rep in one of these categories:

1)   great rep – would hire again without hesitation – wish I could find more like this one
2)   no way – if I had it to do again, would never hire this one
3)   all the rest

Using this as a guide, I'll deploy the category 1 reps first, and into the most important territories, then I'd rank those in category 3 working from the best of them.

I'd begin assigning the reps to the territories in my new worksheet, adjusting pay levels as necessary. When I run out of sales budget, I'll set the rest of the reps aside for later consideration.

Reassigning Accounts

I'd make a tab for each of the chosen reps, and then pull their NBC Ranking report to use as the framework for their newly-configured territories.

Next, I'd distribute the accounts from the excluded reps between the territories.

Then, I'd go back to the territory balancing exercise, creating territory account mixes that can and do deliver NBC levels that support the desired pay rates.

In the territory rebalancing process, there are several things I'd be mindful of:

- ✓ collection of money-making accounts into territories that can produce sufficient NBC to fund target pay packages for the reps
- ✓ removal of small accounts unlikely to be viable with a commission load
- ✓ if necessary, aggregation of money-losing accounts into turnaround territories

As the process of creating viable territories by rebalancing is completed, I'd prepare to terminate reps in category 2, and either terminate or reassign the reps in category 3.

Finito!

At this point, I've done the work of developing a workable plan that will pay appropriately for the profit levels the reps deliver.

The reps can greatly influence their pay by learning about the profit-drivers of the business, and working with the customers to exploit the plan in their favor. Of course, the company will also benefit from changes to the relative efficiency of the customer relationships the reps oversee.

Interestingly, the customers themselves will also see internal profit gains of their own when they do business with the company using fewer of their own resources.

It's a win for everyone.

Conclusion

Successful sales compensation programs require a substantial amount of effort planning and execution, and also a certain level of commitment to bring online.

When they have a clear line to the a good profit strategy, they can be the most powerful tools available for a company to drive substantial gains.

Profit-based plans change the normal sales management dynamic for the better, and in a big way.

I hope the knowledge and tools suggested in this book will set your company on a path to sustained superior profit performance, and make your reps the best-paid in your market.

Acknowledgements

This book, and the work it's based on, wouldn't be possible without the mentoring and assistance of many people.

First, I'd like to thank Dave Cichelli and Bob Conti at the Alexander Group for giving me a grounding in the principles and techniques of advanced sales compensation design. The work done by their firm is first-rate, where they help very large firms address the challenges of sales compensation in complex environments far beyond those contemplated in this book.

Second, I'd like to thank my editor, Joseph Glad, who invested many hours in the raw transcripts for this book. If I seem particularly articulate, it's purely due to his work in untangling my original thoughts, deleting my verbal ticks, and assembling the rough text into something most readers would appreciate.

Finally, Susan Merlo suggested that a book could be a valuable resource for business owners, and shepherded me through the process—again.

Glossary

CoGS—Cost of Goods Sold: purchase cost of product sold to customer as it appears above the Gross Profit line on a P&L statement (may include cost modifiers such as inbound freight and vendor rebates)

CTS—Cost to Serve: total of all operating expenses, excluding: rep-level sales compensation, extraordinary items, and usually non-cash expenses like depreciation

CTS%—percentage of revenue consumed by CTS
(CTS ÷ revenue)

Delta—difference in results (usually profit) from one time period to another (usually year-over-year same period)

GM%—Gross Margin: the percentage of revenue represented by GP
(GP ÷ revenue x 100)

GP—Gross Profit: fraction of revenue remaining after CoGS is deducted
(revenue—CoGS)

LIPA –Line-Item Profit Analytics: using highly granular (usually invoice line-item) profit to evaluate profits or losses in very small increments of transactional business

NBC—Net Before Compensation: profit left after CoGS and CTS are deducted from revenue
(revenue—CoGS—CTS)

NBC%—NBC Rate: percentage of revenue represented by the NBC
(NBC ÷ revenue)

NBT—Net Before Taxes: the company's "bottom line"—earnings the company will pay taxes on
(revenue—CoGS—CTS—sales comp)

Net—Net Profit: net or operating profit remaining after all operating expenses are covered
(revenue—CoGS—CTS—sales compensation)

Net%—Net Profit Rate: percentage of revenue represented by the Net
(Net ÷ revenue)

P&L—Profit and Loss statement: standard financial statement, showing profit made or money lost during a specific time period. I recommend a specific layout that shows NBC.

	Rev (revenue)
−	**CoGS** (Cost of Goods Sold)
=	**GP** (gross profit)
−	**CTS** (Cost-To-Serve or operating expenses)
=	**NBC** (Net Before sales Compensation)
−	Sales Comp
=	**NBT** (Net Before Taxes)

PIP—Peak Internal Profit: the total profit generated by only the money-making invoice lines

QPM—Quantum Profit Management: an advanced management philosophy and practice where very granular profit results are used to drive strategies and tactics that drive large numbers of incremental improvements in profitability

SKU—Stock Keeping Unit: a single, orderable item in your company's selection of products and services offered to customers

Plan Design Workbook

The workbook utilized in the Plan Design Walk-Through chapter of this book can be downloaded from my website.

There are two pairs of workbooks, each with the fully-populated workbook used in the book, and an empty version ready for you to enter your own numbers.

Workbook Set for Excel 2007 and Later

www.randymaclean.com/CompPlanDesign.xlsx
www.randymaclean.com/CompPlanDesign-example.xlsx

Workbook Set for Excel 97-2003

www.randymaclean.com/CompPlanDesign.xls
www.randymaclean.com/CompPlanDesign-example.xls

Walk-Through Chapter on Video

The walk-through chapter is also available as video. You can watch it online at:

www.randymaclean.com/design_walk_thru.asp

WayPoint Analytics

WayPoint Analytics is an online system used by wholesale distribution companies to closely measure and manage their profitability.

WayPoint will hold a rolling three years of your company's invoice data, freshen it on a weekly or monthly basis, and load your quarterly P&L statements. The system distributes all of your expenses throughout the invoices, costing your business out in fine detail.

WayPoint produces hundreds of detailed profit reports— covering every aspect of profit management for every aspect of your business. The reports are accessible via the Internet from your desktop, your home, or on the road on your smart phone or tablet.

WayPoint clients have posted 100%, 300% and 500% profit gains by having the insights given to them through the WayPoint reports into how and where their companies make and lose money. These insights have rendered them free to act to pass their competitors by.

I'd be delighted to discuss your business or answer your questions.

Call us or visit our website at:
www.waypointanalytics.com

About the Author

Randy MacLean is the founder and President of WayPoint Analytics, a software-in-the-cloud company that serves the wholesale distribution industry. An expert in the field of distribution analytics and profitability, Randy is a frequent presenter to wholesale distribution associations across the US and Canada.

He is a co-founder of the Advanced Profit Innovation Conference (APIC), a bi-annual two-day accredited educational conference where the top experts in distribution profitability meet for two days to teach each other, and a selected group for distribution executives, best practices and what's coming next.

Using WayPoint and working with hundreds of business owners and managers, Randy's been focused on providing the deep analytics needed to identify and control the millions of profit increments that exist and are lost in a typical business. He's partnered with Bruce Merrifield, and together they've spent most of the last decade helping distribution executives recognize and capture the enormous, but largely unrealized, profits that exists in every distribution company.

In his off time, Randy is a skilled shooter, an NRA Certified Instructor, and enjoys ballroom dancing with his wife, Diane.

A native of Canada, he's been a resident of Scottsdale, Arizona for over 20 years, where he enjoys year-round summer-style living with his wife, Diane, and their dogs.

To find out more about Randy MacLean, visit him at www.randymaclean.com or www.waypointanalytics.com